50% OFF Online TEAS Course!

Dear Customer,

As a way of showing our appreciation to you, we have partnered with Mometrix Test Preparation to offer **50% off their online TEAS Course.** Many TEAS courses are needlessly expensive and don't deliver enough value. With their course, you get access to the best TEAS prep material, and you only pay half price.

It's mobile friendly and contains over **100 lessons**, **190+ video reviews**, over **2,000+ practice questions**, as well as **300+ flashcards**

Topics Covered:

- Reading
- English & Language Usage
- Science
- Math

Go to this link: mometrix.com/university/teas-test
Discount code: **TBP50**

Questions:
universityhelp@mometrix.com

SCAN HERE

FREE Test Taking Tips Video/DVD Offer

To better serve you, we created videos covering test taking tips that we want to give you for FREE. **These videos cover world-class tips that will help you succeed on your test.**

We just ask that you send us feedback about this product. Please let us know what you thought about it—whether good, bad, or indifferent.

To get your **FREE videos**, you can use the QR code below or email freevideos@studyguideteam.com with "Free Videos" in the subject line and the following information in the body of the email:

    a. The title of your product

    b. Your product rating on a scale of 1-5, with 5 being the highest

    c. Your feedback about the product

If you have any questions or concerns, please don't hesitate to contact us at info@studyguideteam.com.

Thank you!

ATI TEAS 7th Edition Pocket Guide

TEAS Study Prep and
Practice Test Questions
Book for Exam Review

Joshua Rueda

Copyright © 2022 by TPB Publishing

All rights reserved. No part of this publication may be reproduced, distributed, or transmitted in any form or by any means, including photocopying, recording, or other electronic or mechanical methods, without the prior written permission of the publisher, except in the case of brief quotations embodied in critical reviews and certain other noncommercial uses permitted by copyright law.

Written and edited by TPB Publishing.

TPB Publishing is not associated with or endorsed by any official testing organization. TPB Publishing is a publisher of unofficial educational products. All test and organization names are trademarks of their respective owners. Content in this book is included for utilitarian purposes only and does not constitute an endorsement by TPB Publishing of any particular point of view.

Interested in buying more than 10 copies of our product? Contact us about bulk discounts:
bulkorders@studyguideteam.com

ISBN 13: 9781637757239
ISBN 10: 1637757239

Table of Contents

Welcome *1*

FREE Videos/DVD OFFER *2*

Quick Overview *3*

Test-Taking Strategies *4*

Introduction to TEAS 7 .... *6*

Bonus Content *9*

Reading *10*

    Key Ideas and Details 10

    Craft and Structure 24

    Integration of Knowledge and Ideas 36

Mathematics *46*

    Numbers and Algebra 46

    Measurement and Data 72

Science *90*

    Human Anatomy and Physiology 90

    Biology 120

    Chemistry 138

Scientific Reasoning 161

English and Language Usage *172*

   Conventions of Standard English 172

   Knowledge of Language 193

   Using Language and Vocabulary to Express Ideas in Writing 201

Welcome

Dear Reader,

Welcome to your new Test Prep Books pocket guide! We are pleased that you chose us to help you prepare for your exam. There are many study options to choose from, and we appreciate you choosing us. Studying can be a daunting task, but we have designed a smart, effective study guide to help prepare you for what lies ahead.

Whether you're a parent helping your child learn and grow, a high school student working hard to get into your dream college, or a nursing student studying for a complex exam, we want to help give you the tools you need to succeed. We hope this study guide gives you the skills and the confidence to thrive, and we can't thank you enough for allowing us to be part of your journey.

In an effort to continue to improve our products, we welcome feedback from our customers. We look forward to hearing from you. Suggestions, success stories, and criticisms can all be communicated by emailing us at info@studyguideteam.com.

Sincerely,
Test Prep Books Team

FREE Videos/DVD OFFER

Doing well on your exam requires both knowing the test content and understanding how to use that knowledge to do well on the test. We offer completely FREE test taking tip videos. **These videos cover world-class tips that you can use to succeed on your test.**

To get your **FREE videos**, you can use the QR code below or email freevideos@studyguideteam.com with "Free Videos" in the subject line and the following information in the body of the email:

> a. The title of your product
> b. Your product rating on a scale of 1-5, with 5 being the highest
> c. Your feedback about the product

If you have any questions or concerns, please don't hesitate to contact us at info@studyguideteam.com.

Quick Overview

As you draw closer to taking your exam, effective preparation becomes more and more important. Thankfully, you have this study guide to help you get ready.

A large part of the guide is devoted to showing you what content to expect on the exam and to helping you better understand that content. Near the end of this guide is a practice test so that you can see how well you have grasped the content. Then, answer explanations are provided so that you can understand why you missed certain questions.

Once the exam is complete, take some time to relax. Even if you feel that you need to take the exam again, you will be well served by some down time before you begin studying again. It's often easier to convince yourself to study if you know that it will come with a reward!

Test-Taking Strategies

1. Predicting the Answer

When you feel confident in your preparation for a multiple-choice test, try predicting the answer before reading the answer choices. This is especially useful on questions that test objective factual knowledge or that ask you to fill in a blank. By predicting the answer before reading the available choices, you eliminate the possibility that you will be distracted or led astray by an incorrect answer choice.

2. Reading the Whole Question

Too often, test takers scan a multiple-choice question, recognize a few familiar words, and immediately jump to the answer choices. Test authors are aware of this common impatience, and they will sometimes prey upon it.

3. Looking for Wrong Answers

Long and complicated multiple-choice questions can be intimidating. One way to simplify a difficult multiple-choice question is to eliminate all of the answer choices that are clearly wrong. In most sets of answers, there will be at least one selection that can be dismissed right away.

4. Don't Overanalyze

Anxious test takers often overanalyze questions. When you are nervous, your brain will often run wild, causing you to make associations and discover clues that don't actually exist. If you feel that this may be a problem for you, do whatever you can to slow down during the test.

5. Your First Instinct

Many people struggle with multiple-choice tests because they overthink the questions. If you have studied sufficiently for the test, you should be prepared to trust your first instinct once you have carefully and completely read the question and all of the answer choices.

6. Subtle Negatives

One of the oldest tricks in the multiple-choice test writer's book is to subtly reverse the meaning of a question with a word like *not* or *except*. If you are not paying attention to each word in the question, you can easily be led astray by this trick.

Introduction to TEAS 7

Background of the ATI TEAS

The Test of Essential Academic Skills (TEAS) is a standardized test created and distributed by Assessment Technologies Institute (ATI) to examine the test taker's aptitude for skill sets fundamental to a career in nursing. As such, the TEAS is used by nursing schools and allied health schools in the United States and Canada as a chief criterion for admission. The TEAS is currently in its seventh iteration.

Test Administration

The TEAS 7 may be administered by a nursing or allied health school or a PSI testing center. Test takers can register at atitesting.com or directly through the school to which they wish to apply, as most nursing schools offer the test on-campus periodically throughout the year.

Students may retake the TEAS 7, but most schools have limitations such as the number of days students must wait between attempts or the number of attempts students may make in a given period.

Introduction to TEAS 7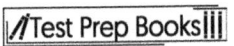

Test Format

The TEAS 7 is comprised of 170 questions. The questions are divided between four subject areas—Reading, Mathematics, Science, and English & Language Usage.

Subject Area	Questions	Time Limit (minutes)
Reading	45	55
Mathematics	38	57
Science	50	60
English & Language Usage	37	37
Total	**170**	**209**

There are five possible question formats: multiple choice with four possible answer choices for each question; multiple-select, where the test taker must select all correct answer options; supply answer or fill-in-the-blank questions; ordering, where the test taker must put items in a list in the correct order; and hot spot, where the test taker will be given an image and must select a certain area of that image.

Scoring

Shortly after the examination, test takers will receive several different numbered scores with their TEAS 7 results. Schools typically look at the Composite Individual Total Score.

Bonus Content

For additional resources, please check out our bonus page by using the link or QR code:

testprepbooks.com/bonus/teas7pocket

Reading

Key Ideas and Details

Summarize a Multi-Paragraph Text

A **summary** is a shortened version of the original text, written by the reader in their own words. In order to effectively summarize a more complex text, it is necessary to fully understand the original source, and to highlight the major points covered. It may be helpful to outline the original text to get a big picture view of it, and to avoid getting bogged down in the minor details.

A **topic** is the subject of the text; it can usually be described in a one- to two-word phrase. The **main idea** is more detailed and provides the author's central point of the text. It can be expressed through a complete sentence and is often found in the beginning, middle, or end of a paragraph.

Supporting details help readers better develop and understand the main idea. Supporting details answer questions like **who, what, where, when, why**, and **how**. Different types of supporting details include examples, facts and statistics, anecdotes, and sensory details.

Reading

Example

Read the following paragraph and then answer the question.

According to the U.S. Department of Health and Human Services, 16 million people in the United States presently suffer from a smoking-related condition, and nearly nine million suffer from a serious smoking-related illness. According to the Centers for Disease Control and Prevention (CDC), tobacco products cause nearly six million deaths per year. This number is projected to rise to over eight million deaths by 2030. Smokers, on average, die ten years earlier than their nonsmoking peers.

Q. Which of the following statements most accurately summarizes the paragraph?
   a. Tobacco is less healthy than many alternatives.
   b. Tobacco is deadly, and smokers would be much better off kicking the addiction.
   c. In the United States, local, state, and federal governments typically tax tobacco products, which leads to high prices.
   d. Tobacco products shorten smokers' lives by ten years and kill more than six million people per year.

Explanation
Answer. B: The author cites disease and deaths associated with smoking. Choice B is the correct answer because it summarizes all the details offered against smoking tobacco.

Make Inferences and Draw Conclusions About a Text's Purpose and Meaning

To **infer a logical conclusion** from a text, readers should actively read the text by making predictions, analyzing facts, and determining key words. From these clues, readers should be able to draw a logical conclusion from the text.

Example
Q. When students use inference, what are they able to do?

    a. Make logical assumptions based on contextual clues
    b. Independently navigate various types of text
    c. Summarize a text's main idea
    d. Paraphrase a text's main idea

Explanation
Answer. A: When a person infers something, he or she is demonstrating the ability to extract key information and make logical assumptions based on that information.

Reading

Demonstrate Comprehension of Written Directions

When presented with a set of directions, readers should start at the very beginning and read the list through carefully before taking any action. This aids in comprehension and ensures that you catch all relevant information. Take your time and reread sentences and passages if necessary.

Example
The next question is based on the following directions.

Follow these instructions in chronological order to transform the word into something new.
> 1. Start with the word LOATHING.
> 2. Eliminate the first and last letter in the starting word.
> 3. Eliminate all the vowels, except I, from the word.
> 4. Eliminate the letter H from the word.

Q. What new word has been spelled?
   a. TON
   b. THIN
   c. TIN
   d. TAN

Explanation

Answer. C: After removing the first and last letter, *OATHIN* remains. Next, we eliminate all the vowels, except *I*, to get *THIN*. Finally, we remove the *H* to get *TIN*; thus, Choice *C* is the correct answer.

Locate Specific Information in a Text

Text features are used to bring clarity or to affect the meaning of a text and include bolding, italics, underlining, formatting, headings, and subheadings.

Usually, **bolding** words indicate key concepts, *italicizing* words indicate another language or an emphasis, and underlining can also indicate a key term. Different color text can be used to make certain parts stand out or to indicate that a new section is beginning.

Formatting—such as indentation or bullet points—helps to clearly present content. Content may also be left justified, centered, or right justified. Text is often centered to stand out and catch the reader's eye.

Headings and subheadings allow the reader to find information quickly. Headings show a complete change in thought. Subheadings, which fall below headings, show different aspects of the same topic.

Reading

Additional textual features in longer pieces of writing that locate specific information within the larger text include a **table of contents**, a **glossary**, and an **index**.

Example:
Read the following paragraph and then answer the question.

Entering Jessica's room, Jessica's mom stepped over a pile of laundry, a stack of magazines, and a pile of dishes. *My messy daughter*, she thought, shaking her head.

Q. Which of the following statements explains the purpose of the italics in the phrase, *My messy daughter*?

    a. The italics represent the key thought of the paragraph.
    b. The italics represent a character's thoughts.
    c. The italics indicate a change of topic.
    d. The italics show which section of a larger work this paragraph is in.

Explanation
Answer. B: The italics are used to make the character's thoughts stand out from the rest of the paragraph.

Reading

Analyze, Interpret, and Apply Information from Charts, Graphs, and Other Visuals

Line Graphs

Line graphs are used to track changes in information over time. They have a horizontal x-axis and a vertical y-axis. Dots are plotted where the x- and y-axes intersect, and the dots are connected into lines. Multiple lines can also be present in a line graph to demonstrate a cluster of subjects.

Example

Use the line graph to answer the following question.

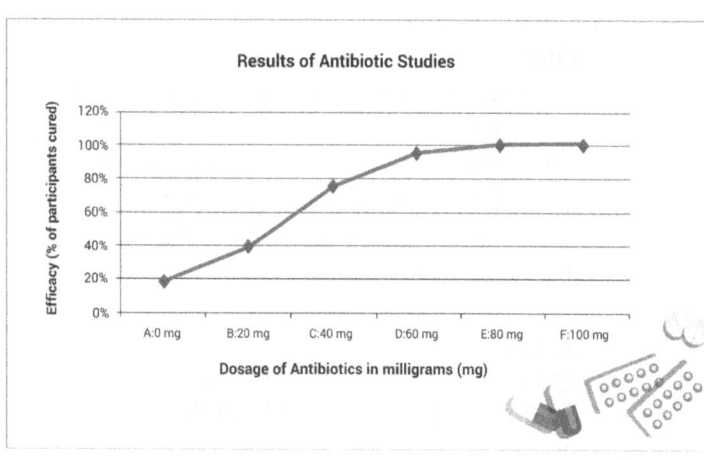

Reading

Q. What percentage of participants cured corresponds with the dosage of 20 mg?

- a. 20%
- b. 40%
- c. 60%
- d. 79%

Explanation

Answer. B: The line graph shows that at 20mg, 40% of patients were cured. The other answer choices are incorrect.

Bar Graphs

Bar graphs are useful for making comparisons between multiple variables. The multiple variables are shown on a horizontal X axis, and the bars themselves rise up on a vertical Y axis.

Reading

Example

The question is based on the following bar graph.

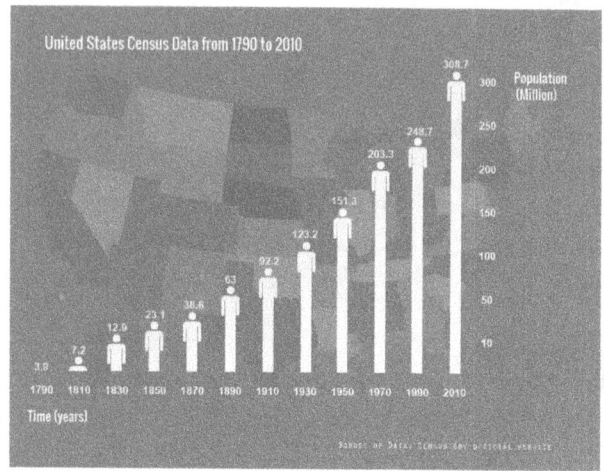

Q. In which of the following years was the United States population less than it was in 1930?
 a. 1950
 b. 1970
 c. 1910
 d. 1990

Explanation

Answer. C: The correct answer is Choice *C*, 1910. There are two ways to arrive at the correct answer. You could find the four answer choices on the graph and compare them, or you could identify that the

Reading

population never decreases from one census to the next. Thus, the correct answer needs to be the only answer choice that is earlier in time than the others, Choice *C*. Choices *A*, *B*, and *D* are incorrect because they are later in time, and thus have a greater population, than the 1930 census.

Pie Chart

A pie chart shows how different categories add up to 100 percent. Each category represents a "slice of the pie," and the round pie chart visually exhibits which slices are bigger or smaller than the others.

Reading

Example

The following question is based on the pie chart.

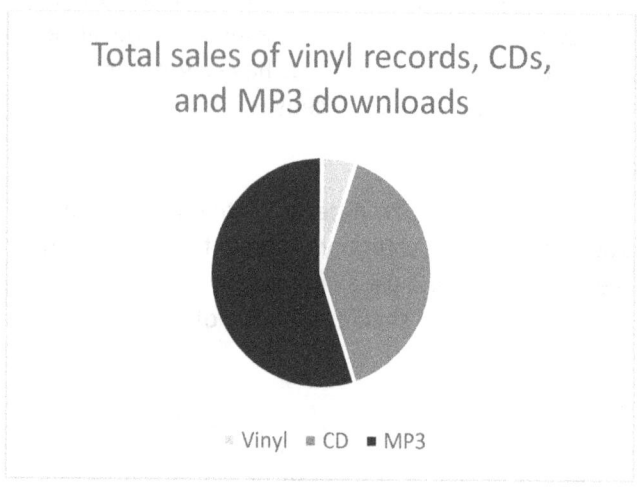

Q. This chart indicates how many sales of CDs, vinyl records, and MP3 downloads occurred over the last year. Approximately what percentage of the total sales was from CDs?

    a. 55%
    b. 25%
    c. 40%
    d. 5%

Explanation

Answer. C: The total percentage of a pie chart equals 100%. We can see that CD sales make up less than half of the chart (50%) and more than a quarter (25%), and the only answer choice that meets these criteria is Choice *C*, 40%.

Legends and Map Keys

Legends and map keys are placed on maps to identify what the symbols on the map represent. Generally, map symbols stand for things like railroads, national or state highways, and public parks. These symbols can usually be found on the bottom right corner of a map. In addition, there may be a compass rose that shows the directions of north, south, east, and west. Most maps are oriented such that the top of the map is north. Scales on maps may also be useful; these show relative distances between fixed points.

Reading

Example

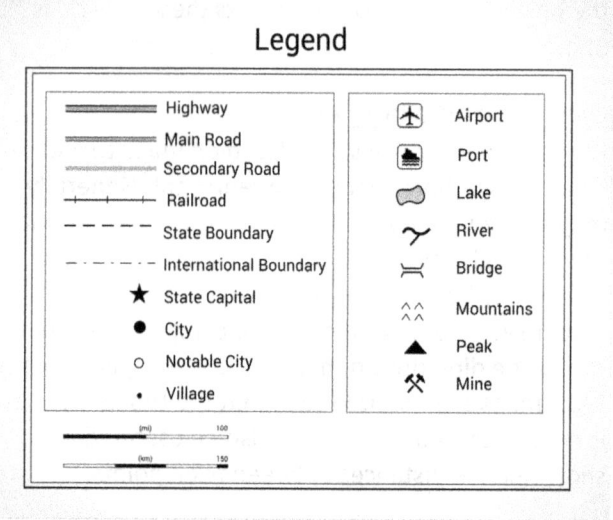

Q. What symbol is used in the legend above to represent mountains?

a. ▲

b. ★

c. ⚒

d. ^^ ^^

Explanation

Answer. D: The map legend uses four ^ symbols to represent mountains.

Interpret Events in a Sequence

Ideas within texts should be organized, connected, or related in some way. In sequential relationships, ideas or events occur in order of time. Every passage has a **plot**, and each plot has a logical order, which is also known as a sequence.

In some cases, sequence can be found through comprehension techniques. For example, more literal passages might number the sequences or use key words such as *firstly*, *secondly*, *finally*, *next*, or *then*.

In most cases, however, readers must correctly order events through inferential and evaluative reading techniques; they have to place events in a logical order without explicit cues. They may also have to use inferences to fill in gaps that are not explicitly stated in the text.

Ideas in a text can also have a **comparative** relationship wherein certain qualities are shown to overlap or be the same between two different things. In comparative relationships, similarities are drawn out.

Passages that have a **cause-and-effect** relationship demonstrate a specific type of connection between ideas or events wherein one (or multiple) caused another. Words such as *if*, *since*, *because*, *then*, or *consequently* indicate a cause-and-effect relationship.

Example
Q. Which best describes the **plot** in fiction?
 a. What happens in the story or the storyline
 b. Character development
 c. The time and place of the story
 d. The events in the story that are true

Explanation
Answer. A: The plot describes what happens in the storyline, or the sequence of events.

Craft and Structure

Distinguish Between Fact and Opinion to Identify Misconceptions and Biases

Fact and Opinion
A **fact** is information that can be proven true, often by scientific experiments, mathematical equations, or corroborating information. If I say $2 + 2 = 5$, this information can be disproven, because the equation $2 + 2 = 4$ can be proven true.

Opinions are statements that are debatable and cannot be proven or disproven. Examples of opinions include subjective topics such as morals, rights, and values.

Biases and Stereotypes

A **bias** is an individual prejudice that ignores evidence contrary to the belief. To prefer people who wear green hats to people who wear purple hats is to hold a favorable bias toward people who wear green hats. Biases can be favorable or unfavorable.

A **stereotype** is a widely held belief projected onto an entire group. Those who make stereotypes fail to consider individuals within the group and how they might differentiate from that group.

Stereotypes and biases can both be harmful toward the groups they target.

Tone

Tone refers to the writer's attitude toward the subject matter. For example, the tone conveys how the writer feels about the characters and their circumstances in a work of fiction. A neutral tone, often used in nonfiction, demonstrates that the writer is presenting a topic impartially.

Example

Q. Which of the following is an opinion, rather than historical fact?

  a. Leif Erikson was definitely the son of Erik the Red; however, historians debate the year of his birth.
  b. Leif Erikson's crew called the land Vinland since it was plentiful with grapes.
  c. Leif Erikson deserves more credit for his contributions in exploring the New World.
  d. Leif Erikson explored the Americas nearly five hundred years before Christopher Columbus.

Explanation

Answer. C: Choice *C* is the correct answer; it is the author's opinion that Erikson deserves more credit, not a verifiable fact.

Interpret the Meaning of Words and Phrases Using Context

Context, or surrounding words, gives clues as to what unknown words mean.

Context clues help readers understand unfamiliar words. Below are the different types of context clues.

Reading

- A **synonym** is a word that has the same meaning as another word. Example: <u>Large</u> boxes are needed to pack <u>big</u> items.

- An **antonym** is a word that has the opposite definition of another word. Example: <u>Large</u> boxes are not needed to pack <u>small</u> items.

- **Definitions** are sometimes included within a sentence to define uncommon words. Example: They practiced the <u>rumba</u>, a <u>type of dance</u>, for hours on end.

- **Explanations** provide context through elaboration. Example: Large boxes holding items weighing over sixty pounds were stacked in the corner.

- **Contrast** in a sentence helps readers to know that the unfamiliar word is set in contrast to a familiar one. Example: These <u>minute</u> creatures were much different than the <u>huge</u> mammals that the zoologist was accustomed to dealing with.

<u>Example</u>
The next question is based on the following sentence.

As the tour group approached the bottom of Chichen Itza, the prodigious Mayan pyramid, they became nervous about climbing its distant peak.

Q. Based on the context of the preceding sentence, which of the following words shows the correct meaning of the word *prodigious*?
   a. Very large
   b. Famous
   c. Very old
   d. Fancy

Explanation
Answer. A: The word *prodigious* is defined as very impressive, amazing, or large. In this sentence, the meaning can be drawn from the words *they became nervous about climbing its distant peak*, as this would be an appropriate reaction upon seeing a very large peak that's far in the distance.

Connotation and Denotation
The **connotative** meaning of a word is not the literal definition, but rather what the word implies or the ideas or feelings a word invokes. For example, calling a person *warm* implies they are friendly and welcoming, not that they operate at a moderate temperature (the dictionary definition of warm). Words can imply much more than their literal definitions.

Reading

The **denotative** meaning of a word is a word's literal or exact definition. The denotative meaning of a word is the one you would find in a dictionary.

Example
The question below is based on the following sentence.

Xavier *propagated* his belief that dragons were real to his friends gathered around the campfire.

Q. Which of the following words is the denotative form of the word *propagate?*
    a. Whispered
    b. Expressed
    c. Persuaded
    d. Shouted

Explanation
Answer. B: To *propagate* means to spread, disseminate, promote, or otherwise make known an idea, thought, or belief. The denotative form of a word is the literal definition of the word.

Figurative Language
Similes and **metaphors** are types of figurative language that compare two things, but their formats differ. A simile says that two things are similar and makes a comparison using "like" or "as"—A is like B, or A is as [some characteristic] as B—whereas a

metaphor states that two things are exactly the same—A is B.

Alliteration and **assonance** are both varieties of sound repetition. Other types of sound repetition include **anaphora**—repetition that occurs at the beginning of the sentences; **epiphora**—repetition occurring at the end of phrases; **antimetabole**—repetition of words in a succession; **antiphrasis**—a form of denial of an assertion in a text; **onomatopoeia**—words whose spelling mimics the sound they describe; and a **pun**—a play on words based on the same or similar pronunciation.

Example

Q: Which of the following is NOT an example of onomatopoeia?
- a. Crash
- b. Drop
- c. Bang
- d. Sizzle

Explanation

Answer. B: Drop is a verb meaning to fall; it does not describe the sound of an object falling.

Evaluate the Author's Purpose in a Given Text

Authors write in order to persuade, entertain, inform, express feelings, or a combination of these. Readers may need to utilize critical thinking and logical reasoning to infer what an author's purpose is. Readers should also take note of the author's tone and incorporate that into their analysis of the text.

There are four main types of writing: narrative, expository, descriptive, and persuasive.

Narrative writing: When an author writes a narrative, they are telling a story. Narratives develop characters, drive a sequence of events, and deal with conflict. Examples of classic narratives are *The Great Gatsby*, *One Hundred Years of Solitude*, and *Song of Solomon*.

Expository writing: Expository writing is meant to instruct or inform and usually lacks any kind of persuasive elements. Expository writing includes recipes, academic lessons, repair manuals, or newspaper articles. Expository writing in academia uses third-person point of view and strives to be non-biased in its presentation.

Descriptive writing: Descriptive writing is writing that uses imagery and figurative language to allow the reader to feel as if they are experiencing the text firsthand. For example, a descriptive paragraph about Heather eating an ice cream cone will detail the smooth cream dripping down the cone, the crunch of the waffle cone, and the coldness and sweetness of the first bite. The reader feels the experience through the author's sensory language.

Persuasive writing: Persuasive writing is used when someone is writing an argument. Authors using persuasive writing are attempting to change the opinions and attitudes of their audience. Good persuasive writing will use credible sources and thoughtful analysis, stating both sides of the argument without bias.

Example
Q. Which type of writing is meant to instruct of inform?
- a. Descriptive writing
- b. Narrative writing
- c. Persuasive writing
- d. Expository writing

Explanation
Answer. D: Expository writing is meant to instruct or inform. Expository writing does not tell a story, persuade the author, or rely only on descriptive language to get its point across.

Evaluate the Author's Point of View or Perspective in a Given Text

An author's **point of view** is the perspective from which the author writes. The author may write with a sole perspective, or they may present more than one.

First-person: The story is told from the perspective of the writer or of a single character. First-person point of view uses personal pronouns such as *I*, *me*, *we*, *us*, *our*, *my*, and *myself*. First-person point of view shows the character's innermost thoughts.

Second-person: This point of view isn't commonly used in fiction or nonfiction writing because it directly addresses the audience using the pronouns *you*, *your*, and *yourself*. Second-person perspective is more appropriate in direct communication, such as business letters or emails.

Third-person: Third-person uses the pronouns *he*, *she*, *they*, and *it* and is appropriate for a formal essay where the focus should be on the subject matter, not the writer or the reader.

In fiction writing, third-person point of view can be limited, omniscient, or objective.

Third-person limited: The story is told by a narrator who has access to the thoughts and feelings of just one character.

Third-person omniscient: The narrator knows the thoughts and emotions of all the characters.

Third-person objective: The narrator has access to the characters' actions and words but does not have access to their thoughts and feelings.

Evaluating the Credibility of a Print or Digital Source

Recognizing the perspective from which an author writes is also a critical element of evaluating the author's credibility. Other elements to consider when evaluating a source are the publisher, any noticeable bias, the references the author provides, the accuracy/reliability of the work, and the coverage of the topic.

Reading

Example

Q. Which of the following sentences uses second person point of view?

    a. I don't want to make plans for the weekend before I see my work schedule.

    b. She had to miss the last three yoga classes due to illness.

    c. Pluto is no longer considered a planet because it is not gravitationally dominant.

    d. Be sure to turn off all of the lights before locking up for the night.

Explanation

Answer. D: Choice *D* directly addresses the reader, so it is in second person point of view. This is an imperative sentence since it issues a command; imperative sentences have an understood you as the subject. Choice *A* uses first person pronouns I and my. Choices *B* and *C* are incorrect because they use third person point of view.

Integration of Knowledge and Ideas

Use Evidence from the Text to Make Predictions, Inferences, and Draw Conclusions

Predictions

Some texts use suspense and foreshadowing to captivate readers. Authors often build suspense and add depth and meaning to a work by leaving clues to provide hints or predict future events in the story; this is called foreshadowing. While some instances of foreshadowing are subtle, others are quite obvious.

Inferences

Making an **inference** requires the reader to read between the lines and look for what is implied rather than what is directly stated. Using information that is known from the text, the reader is able to make a logical assumption about information that is not explicitly stated but is probably true. Authors employ literary devices such as tone, characterization, and theme to engage the audience by showing details of the story instead of merely telling them.

Conclusions

Active readers should also draw conclusions. When doing so, the reader should ask the following questions: What is this text about? What does the author believe? Does this text have merit? Do I believe the author? Would this text support my argument? Always read cautiously and critically. Interact with text and record reactions in the margins. These active reading skills help determine the author's purpose as well as the reader's own conclusion about the text.

Example

Q. Which of the following statements would make the best conclusion to an essay about civil rights activist Rosa Parks?

    a. On December 1, 1955, Rosa Parks refused to give up her bus seat to a white passenger, setting in motion the Montgomery bus boycott.

    b. Rosa Parks was a hero to many and came to symbolize the way that ordinary people could bring about real change in the Civil Rights Movement.

    c. Rosa Parks died in 2005 in Detroit, having moved from Montgomery shortly after the bus boycott.

    d. Rosa Parks' arrest was an early part of the Civil Rights Movement and helped lead to the passage of the Civil Rights Act of 1964.

Explanation

Answer. B: Choice *A*, Choice *C*, and Choice *D* all relate facts but do not present the kind of general statement that would serve as an effective conclusion. Choice *B* is correct.

Compare and Contrast the Themes Expressed in One or More Texts

The **theme** is the central message of a fictional work, whether that work is prose, drama, or poetry. It is the heart of what an author is trying to say to readers through the writing, and theme is largely conveyed through literary elements and techniques.

How Authors Develop Theme

Authors employ a variety of techniques to present a theme. They may compare or contrast characters, events, places, ideas, or historical or invented settings to speak thematically. They may use analogies, metaphors, similes, allusions, or other literary devices to convey the theme. An author's use of diction, syntax, and tone can also help convey the theme. Authors will often develop themes through the development of characters, use of the setting, repetition of ideas, use of symbols, and through contrasting value systems. Authors of both fiction and

Reading

nonfiction genres will use a variety of these techniques to develop one or more themes.

Cultural Influence on Themes

Certain themes are universal to the human condition, including birth, death, marriage, friendship, finding meaning, etc. However, different cultures have different norms and general beliefs concerning these themes. Readers must avoid being **ethnocentric**, which means believing the aspects of one's own culture to be superior to that of other cultures.

Example

Q. Read the following poem. Which option best expresses the symbolic meaning of the "road" and the overall theme?

> Two roads diverged in a yellow wood,
> And sorry I could not travel both
> And be one traveler, long I stood
> And looked down one as far as I could
> To where it bent in the undergrowth;
>
> Then took the other, as just as fair,
> And having perhaps the better claim,
> Because it was grassy and wanted wear;
> Though as for that the passing there
> Had worn them really about the same,
>
> And both that morning equally lay

> In leaves no step had trodden black.
> Oh, I kept the first for another day!
> Yet knowing how way leads on to way,
> I doubted if I should ever come back.
>
> I shall be telling this with a sigh
> Somewhere ages and ages hence:
> Two roads diverged in a wood, and I—
> I took the one less traveled by,
> And that has made all the difference
> —Robert Frost, "The Road Not Taken"

a. A divergent spot where the traveler had to choose the correct path to his destination
b. A choice between good and evil that the traveler needs to make
c. The traveler's struggle between his lost love and his future prospects
d. Life's journey and the choices with which humans are faced

Explanation

Answer. D: Choice *D* correctly summarizes Frost's theme of life's journey and the choices one makes. While Choice *A* can be seen as an interpretation, it is a literal one and is not the overall theme. Literal is not symbolic. Choice *B* presents the idea of good and evil as a theme, and the poem does not specify this struggle for the traveler. Choice *C* is a similarly incorrect answer. Love is not the theme.

Evaluate an Argument

The author's **credibility** is important to an argument: who is the author and what credentials do they have in relation to their topic? Is their writing clean, organized, and unbiased?

It's important to evaluate the author's supporting details to be sure that the details are credible, provide evidence of the author's point, and directly support the main idea.

The **evidence** an author uses must be credible as well; check where the sources came from. Is the date relevant, and are the sources from noteworthy articles or peer-reviewed journals? In order to draw a conclusion from evidence, it's important to examine the credibility and validity of that evidence as well as how (and if) it relates to the main idea.

Next, what type (or combination) of **rhetorical devices** and **appeal** is the author using? Is it an appeal to logic (**logos**), emotion (**pathos**), or credibility and trustworthiness (**ethos**)?

Finally, has the author presented any counterarguments to show the opposition's side? A strong argument considers the opposition and finds a way to refute it. **Counterarguments** show that the author is nonbiased and has explored every avenue possible.

Example

Q. Which of the following statements least supports the argument that the American economy is healthy?

   a. The United States' Gross Domestic Product (GDP), which is the measure of all the goods and services produced in a country, increased by two percent last year.
   b. Unemployment is the lowest it's been in over a decade due to a spike in job creation.
   c. Average household income just hit a historical high point for the twentieth consecutive quarter.
   d. Last year, the output of the United States' manufacturing sector decreased despite repeated massive investments by both the private and public sectors.

Explanation

Answer D: We are looking for the claim that is least supportive of the argument that the American economy is healthy. Choice *A* says that the GDP increased by 2% last year, which supports a claim of health. Choice *B* relays that unemployment is the lowest it's been in over a decade, a sign of a strong economy. Choice *C* states that average household income is at a historical high point. In contrast, the final choice draws a negative conclusion about the economy—a decrease in output even after investments—therefore, a declining manufacturing sector is least supportive that the economy is healthy. Choice *D* is the correct answer.

Evaluate and Integrate Data from Multiple Sources Across Various Formats, Including Media

In order to be relevant, information needs to be specific, reliable, and credible (or trustworthy).

Primary sources are records or items that serve as historical evidence that were created during the time period which they reference. Examples of primary sources include diaries, newspaper articles, speeches, government documents, photographs, and historical artifacts

Secondary sources, such as websites, history books, databases, or reviews, contain analysis or commentary on primary sources. Secondary sources borrow information from primary sources through the process of quoting, summarizing, or paraphrasing.

Constructing Arguments Through Evidence

Using only one form of supporting evidence is not nearly as effective as using a **variety of evidence** to support a claim. Another key aspect of supporting evidence is a **reliable source**.

Logical Sequence

Even if the writer includes plenty of information to support their point, the writing is only effective when the information is in a **logical sequence**.

Integrate Data

It's important to find multiple relevant and credible sources for data. Multiple sources and multiple types of sources help provide a more thorough and balanced perspective. Always consider the data from one source or type of source in light of data from other sources.

Example

Q. First-hand accounts of an event, subject matter, time period, or an individual are referred to as what type of source?

    a. Primary sources
    b. Secondary sources
    c. Direct sources
    d. Indirect sources

Reading

Explanation

Answer. A: Firsthand accounts are given by primary sources—individuals who provide personal or expert accounts of an event, subject matter, time period, or of an individual.

Mathematics

Numbers and Algebra

Convert Among Non-Negative Fractions, Decimals, and Percentages

Decimals and Percentages

A **decimal number** is a number written out with a decimal point instead of as a fraction, for example, 1.25 instead of $\frac{5}{4}$. To convert a percentage to a decimal, move the decimal point two places to the left and remove the % sign. To convert a decimal to a percentage, move the decimal point two places to the right and add a % sign. Here are some examples:

$$65\% = 0.65$$
$$0.33 = 33\%$$
$$0.215 = 21.5\%$$

Fractions and Percentages

Think of percentages as fractions with a denominator of 100. A percentage can be converted to a fraction by

Mathematics

making the number in the percentage the numerator and putting 100 as the denominator:

$$43\% = \frac{43}{100}$$

$$97\% = \frac{97}{100}$$

To convert a fraction to a percent, divide the numerator by the denominator to get a decimal:

$$\frac{9}{12} = 0.75$$

Then convert the decimal to a percentage:

$$0.75 = 75\%$$

Fractions and Decimals

To convert a fraction to a decimal, divide the numerator by the denominator:

$$\frac{5}{20} = 0.25$$

Another option is to multiply the numerator and denominator by whatever is needed to make the denominator equal to 100:

$$\frac{5}{20} \times \frac{5}{5} = \frac{25}{100}$$

When the denominator is equal to 100, the numerator can be turned into a decimal directly:

$$\frac{25}{100} = 0.25$$

To convert a fraction to a decimal, follow the same logic:

$$0.65 = \frac{65}{100}$$

Then you can simplify, if possible:

$$\frac{65}{100} = \frac{13}{20}$$

Mathematics

Example

Q. Express the solution to the following problem in decimal form:

$$\frac{3}{5} \times \frac{7}{10} \div \frac{1}{2}$$

a. 0.042
b. 84%
c. 0.84
d. 0.42

Explanation

Answer. C: Separate this problem first by solving the division operation of the last two fractions. When dividing one fraction by another, invert or flip the second fraction and then multiply the numerators and denominators.

$$\frac{7}{10} \times \frac{2}{1} = \frac{14}{10}$$

Next, multiply the first fraction by this value:

$$\frac{3}{5} \times \frac{14}{10} = \frac{42}{50}$$

In this instance, to find the decimal form, we can multiply the numerator and denominator by 2 to get 100 in the denominator.

$$\frac{42}{50} \times \frac{2}{2} = \frac{84}{100}$$

In decimal form, this would be expressed as 0.84.

Perform Arithmetic Operations with Rational Numbers (Including Positive and Negative Numbers)

Addition

Addition is the combination of two numbers so that their quantities are added together into a cumulative value called a sum. The sign for an addition operation is the + symbol. For example, $9 + 6 = 15$. The 9 and 6 combine to achieve the sum of 15. Addition holds the commutative property, which means that the order of the numbers in an addition equation can be switched without altering the result. Addition also holds the associative property, which means that the grouping of numbers doesn't matter in an addition problem.

Subtraction

Subtraction is taking away one number from another so that their quantities are reduced. The sign designating a subtraction operation is the – symbol,

Mathematics

and the result is called the difference. For example, $9 - 6 = 3$. The number *6* detracts from the number *9* to reach the difference *3*. Unlike addition, subtraction follows neither the commutative nor associative properties. The order and grouping in subtraction impact the result.

When working through subtraction problems involving larger numbers, it's necessary to regroup the numbers. Let's work through a practice problem using regrouping:

$$\begin{array}{r} 3\,2\,5 \\ -\,7\,7 \\ \hline \end{array}$$

Here, it is clear that the ones and tens columns for 77 are greater than the ones and tens columns for 325. To subtract this number, borrow from the tens and hundreds columns. When borrowing from a column, subtracting 1 from the lender column will add 10 to the borrower column:

$$\begin{array}{r} 3\text{-}1\ \ 10+2\text{-}1\ \ 10+5 \\ -\qquad 7\qquad 7 \\ \hline \end{array} = \begin{array}{r} 2\ \ 11\ \ 15 \\ -\ \ \ \ 7\ \ \ 7 \\ \hline 2\ \ \ 4\ \ \ 8 \end{array}$$

After ensuring that each digit in the top row is greater than the digit in the corresponding bottom row, subtraction can proceed as normal, and the answer is found to be 248.

Multiplication

Multiplication involves adding together multiple copies of a number. It is indicated by an × symbol or a number immediately outside of a parenthesis.

The two numbers being multiplied together are called factors, and their result is called a product. For example, $9 \times 6 = 54$. This can be shown alternatively by expansion of either the 9 or the 6:

$$9 \times 6 = 9 + 9 + 9 + 9 + 9 + 9 = 54$$

$$9 \times 6 = 6 + 6 + 6 + 6 + 6 + 6 + 6 + 6 + 6 = 54$$

Like addition, multiplication holds the commutative and associative properties.

Multiplication also follows the distributive property, which allows the multiplication to be distributed through parentheses. The formula for distribution is $a \times (b + c) = ab + ac$.

Division

The signs designating a division operation are the ÷ and / symbols. In division, the second number divides into the first. The number before the division sign is called the dividend or, if expressed as a fraction, the numerator. For example, in $a \div b$, a is the dividend, while in $\frac{a}{b}$, a is the numerator. The number after the division sign is called the divisor or, if expressed as a fraction, the denominator. For example, in $a \div b$, b is the divisor, while in $\frac{a}{b}$, b is the denominator. If a divisor doesn't divide into a dividend evenly, whatever is left over is termed the remainder.

Like subtraction, division doesn't follow the commutative property, as it matters which number comes before the division sign, and division doesn't follow the associative or distributive properties for the same reason.

Exponents

An exponent is an operation used as shorthand for a number multiplied or divided by itself for a defined number of times:

$$3^7 = 3 \times 3 \times 3 \times 3 \times 3 \times 3 \times 3$$

In this example, the 3 is called the base, and the 7 is called the exponent.

The **Zero Power Rule** finds that any number raised to the zero power equals 1. For example, 100^0, 2^0, $(-3)^0$ and 0^0 all equal 1 because the bases are raised to the zero power.

Exponents can be negative. With negative exponents, the equation is expressed as a fraction:

$$3^{-7} = \frac{1}{3^7} = \frac{1}{3 \times 3 \times 3 \times 3 \times 3 \times 3 \times 3}$$

The **Power Rule** concerns exponents being raised by another exponent. When this occurs, the exponents are multiplied by each other:

$$(x^2)^3 = x^6 = (x^3)^2$$

When multiplying two exponents with the same base, the **Product Rule** requires that the base remains the same, and the exponents are added:

$$a^x \times a^y = a^{x+y}$$

When dividing two exponents with the same base, the **Quotient Rule** requires that the base remains the same, but the exponents are subtracted:

$$a^x \div a^y = a^{x-y}$$

1 raised to any power is still equal to 1, and any number raised to the power of 1 is equal to itself. In other words, $a^1 = a$.

Roots

The **square root symbol** is expressed as $\sqrt{}$ and is commonly known as the radical. Finding the square

Mathematics

root of a number is the opposite of finding an exponent, as the operation seeks a number that when multiplied by itself equals the number in the square root symbol. For example, $\sqrt{36} = 6$ because 6 multiplied by 6 equals 36.

Order of Operations

When solving equations with multiple operations, special rules apply. These rules are known as the **Order of Operations**. The order is as follows: Parentheses, Exponents, Multiplication and Division from left to right, and Addition and Subtraction from left to right.

Positive and Negative Numbers

Signs

Aside from 0, numbers can be either positive or negative. The sign for a positive number is the plus sign or the + symbol, while the sign for a negative number is the minus sign or the − symbol. If a number has no designation, then it's assumed to be positive.

Absolute Values

Both positive and negative numbers are valued according to their distance from 0 along a number line. Both 3 and −3 are three spaces from 0. Thus, both −3 and 3 have an absolute value of 3 since they're both three spaces away from 0.

An absolute number is written by placing | | around the number. So, |3| and |−3| both equal 3, as that's their common absolute value.

Example
Q. What is $4 \times 7 + (25 - 21)^2 \div 2$?
   a. 512
   b. 36
   c. 60.5
   d. 22

Explanation
Answer. B: To solve this correctly, keep in mind the order of operations with the mnemonic PEMDAS (Please Excuse My Dear Aunt Sally). This stands for Parentheses, Exponents, Multiplication, Division, Addition, Subtraction. Taking it step by step, solve inside the parentheses first:

$$4 \times 7 + (4)^2 \div 2$$

Then, apply the exponent:

$$4 \times 7 + 16 \div 2$$

Multiplication and division are both performed next:

$$28 + 8$$

Addition and subtraction are done last.

$$28 + 8 = 36$$

The solution is 36.

Compare and Order Rational Numbers (Including Positive and Negative Numbers)

A common question type asks to order rational numbers from least to greatest or greatest to least. The numbers will come in a variety of formats, including decimals, percentages, roots, fractions, and whole numbers.

Whether the question asks to order the numbers from greatest to least or least to greatest, the crux of the question is the same—convert the numbers into a common format. Generally, it's easiest to write the numbers as whole numbers and decimals so they can be placed on a number line.

Example

Q. Arrange the following numbers from least to greatest value:

$$\sqrt{36}, 0.65, 78\%, \frac{3}{4}, 7, 90\%, \frac{5}{2}$$

a. $\frac{5}{2}, 0.65, \sqrt{36}, \frac{3}{4}, 90\%, 78\%, 7$

b. $78\%, \frac{3}{4}, 7, 0.65, \sqrt{36}, 90\%, \frac{5}{2}$

c. $7, \sqrt{36}, \frac{5}{2}, 90\%, 78\%, \frac{3}{4}, 0.65$

d. $\sqrt{36}, \frac{3}{4}, 78\%, 7, 90\%, \frac{5}{2}, 0.65$

Explanation

Answer. C: Of the seven numbers, the whole number (7) and decimal (0.65) are already in an accessible form, so concentrate on the other five.

First, the square root of 36 equals 6. (If the test asks for the root of a non-perfect root, determine which two whole numbers the root lies between.) Next, convert the percentages to decimals. A percentage means "per hundred," so this conversion requires moving the decimal point two places to the left, leaving 0.78 and 0.9. Lastly, evaluate the fractions:

$$\frac{3}{4} = \frac{75}{100} = 0.75 \; ; \frac{5}{2} = 2\frac{1}{2} = 2.5$$

Mathematics

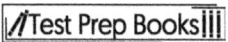

Now, the only step left is to list the numbers in the request order, from greatest to least:

$$7, \sqrt{36}, \frac{5}{2}, 90\%, 78\%, \frac{3}{4}, 0.65$$

Solve Equations with One Variable

Solving equations with one variable is the process of isolating a variable on one side of the equation. The letters in an equation are **variables** as they stand for unknown quantities that you are trying to solve for. The numbers attached to the variables by multiplication are called **coefficients**. X is commonly used as a variable, though any letter can be used. For example, in $3x - 7 = 20$, the variable is $3x$, and it needs to be isolated. The numbers (also called **constants**) are -7 and 20. That means $3x$ needs to be on one side of the equals sign (either side is fine), and all the numbers need to be on the other side of the equals sign.

To accomplish this, the equation must be manipulated by performing **opposite operations** (or **inverse operations**) of what already exists. Remember that addition and subtraction are opposites and that multiplication and division are opposites. Any action taken to one side of the equation must be taken on the other side to maintain equality.

Example

Q. What is the value of b in this equation?
$$5b - 4 = 2b + 17$$

a. 13
b. 24
c. 7
d. 21

Explanation

Answer. C: To solve for the value of b, isolate the variable b on one side of the equation.

Start by moving the lower value of -4 to the other side by adding 4 to both sides:

$$5b - 4 = 2b + 17$$

$$5b - 4 + 4 = 2b + 17 + 4$$

$$5b = 2b + 21$$

Then subtract $2b$ from both sides:

$$5b - 2b = 2b + 21 - 2b$$

$$3b = 21$$

Mathematics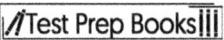

Then divide both sides by 3 to get the value of b:

$$\frac{3b}{3} = \frac{21}{3}$$

$$b = 7$$

Solve Real-World Problems Using One- or Multi-Step Operations with Real Numbers

The key to answering word problems is to translate the words into a math problem. Always keep in mind what the question is asking and what operations could lead to that answer. When a balance is increased, use addition. When a balance is decreased, use subtraction. Common sense and organization are your greatest assets when answering word problems.

Example
Q. If Sarah reads at an average rate of 21 pages in four nights, how long will it take her to read 140 pages?
    a. 6 nights
    b. 26 nights
    c. 8 nights
    d. 27 nights

Explanation

Answer. D: This problem can be solved by setting up a proportion involving the given information and the unknown value. The proportion is:

$$\frac{21 \text{ pages}}{4 \text{ nights}} = \frac{140 \text{ pages}}{x \text{ nights}}$$

We can cross-multiply to get $21x = 4 \times 140$. Solving this, we find $x \approx 26.67$. Since this is not an integer, we round up to 27 nights. 26 nights would not give Sarah enough time.

Solve Real World Problems Involving Percentages

Questions dealing with percentages almost always come in three varieties. The first type will ask to find what percentage of some number will equal another number. The second asks to determine what number is some percentage of another given number. The third will ask what number another number is a given percentage of.

One of the most important parts of correctly answering percentage word problems is to identify the numerator and the denominator. This fraction can then be converted into a percentage.

Mathematics

Problems dealing with percentages may involve an original value, a change in that value, and a percentage change. A problem will provide two pieces of information and ask to find the third. To do so, this formula is used:

$$\frac{change}{original\ value} \times 100 = \text{percent change}.$$

Example

Q. A student gets an 85% on a test with 20 questions. How many answers did the student solve correctly?
- a. 15
- b. 16
- c. 17
- d. 18

Explanation

Answer. C: 85% of a number means that number should be multiplied by 0.85: $0.85 \times 20 = \frac{85}{100} \times \frac{20}{1}$, which can be simplified to $\frac{17}{20} \times \frac{20}{1} = 17$.

Apply Estimation Strategies and Rounding Rules to Real-World Problems

Estimation

Estimation is finding a value that is close to a solution but is not the exact answer. For example, if there are values in the thousands to be multiplied, then each value can be estimated to the nearest thousand and the calculation performed.

Rounding Numbers

It's often convenient to **round a number**, which means giving an approximate figure to make it easier to compare amounts or perform mental math. Round up when the digit is 5 or more. The digit used to determine the rounding, and all subsequent digits, become 0, and the selected place value is increased by 1. Round down when rounding on any digit that is below 5. The rounded digit, and all subsequent digits, become 0, and the preceding digit stays the same.

Determine the Reasonableness of Results

When solving math word problems, the solution obtained should make sense within the given scenario. The step of checking the solution will reduce the possibility of a calculation error or a solution that may be mathematically correct but not applicable in the real world.

Mental Math Estimation

Once a result is determined to be logical within the context of a given problem, the result should be evaluated by its nearness to the expected answer. This is performed by approximating given values to perform mental math. Numbers should be rounded to the nearest value possible to check the initial results.

Example

A customer is buying a new sound system for their home. The customer purchases a stereo for $435, 2 speakers for $67 each, and the necessary cables for $12. The customer chooses an option that allows him to spread the costs over equal payments for 4 months. How much will the monthly payments be? _____

Explanation

After making calculations for the problem, a student determines that the monthly payment will be $145.25. To check the accuracy of the results, the student rounds each cost to the nearest ten ($440 + 70 + 70 + 10$) and determines that the total is approximately $590. Dividing by 4 months gives an approximate monthly payment of $147.50. Therefore, the student can conclude that the solution of $145.25 is very close to what should be expected.

Solve Real World Problems Involving Proportions

A **relationship** is represented by the equation $Y = kX$. X and Y are proportional because as value of X increases, the value of Y also increases. A relationship that is inversely proportional can be represented by the equation $Y = \frac{k}{X}$, where the value of Y decreases as the value of X increases and vice versa.

Proportional reasoning can be used to solve problems involving ratios, percentages, and averages. Ratios can be used in setting up proportions and solving them to find unknowns. For example, if a student completes an average of 10 pages of math homework in 3 nights, how long would it take the student to complete 22 pages? Both ratios can be written as fractions. The second ratio would contain the unknown.

Example
Q. In Jim's school, there are 3 girls for every 2 boys. There are 650 students in total. Using this information, how many students are girls?

    a. 260
    b. 130
    c. 65
    d. 390

Explanation
Answer. D: Three girls for every two boys can be expressed as a ratio: 3 ∶ 2. This can be visualized as splitting the school into 5 groups: 3 girl groups and 2 boy groups. The number of students that are in each

Mathematics

group can be found by dividing the total number of students by 5:

$$\frac{650 \text{ students}}{5 \text{ groups}} = \frac{130 \text{ students}}{\text{group}}$$

To find the total number of girls, multiply the number of students per group (130) by the number of girl groups in the school (3). This equals 390, Choice *D*.

Solve Real-World Problems Involving Ratios and Rates of Change

Ratios

Ratios are used to show the relationship between two quantities. The ratio of oranges to apples in the grocery store may be 3 to 2. That means that for every 3 oranges, there are 2 apples. This comparison can be expanded to represent the actual number of oranges and apples, such as 36 oranges to 24 apples.

Unit Rate

Rates are used to compare two quantities with different units. **Unit rates** are the simplest form of rate. With unit rates, the denominator in the comparison of two units is one. For example, if someone can type at a rate of 1000 words in 5 minutes, then their unit rate for typing is $\frac{1000}{5} = 200$ words in one minute or 200 words per minute. Any rate can be converted into a unit rate by dividing to make the denominator one.

Conversion Factor
Ratios and rates can be used together to convert rates into different units. For example, if someone is driving 50 kilometers per hour, that rate can be converted into miles per hour by using a ratio known as the **conversion factor**.

Scale Factor
The ratio between two similar geometric figures is called the **scale factor**.

Rate of Change
Rate of change for any line calculates the steepness of the line over a given interval. Rate of change is also known as the slope, or $\frac{rise}{run}$. The TEAS will focus on the rate of change for linear functions which are straight lines. The slope is given by the change in y divided by the change in x.

So, the formula looks like this:

$$slope = \frac{y_2 - y_1}{x_2 - x_1}$$

Mathematics

Given the Slope and y-Intercept

Linear equations are commonly written in slope-intercept form, $y = mx + b$, where m represents the slope of the line and b represents the y-intercept. The slope is the rate of change between the variables, usually expressed as a whole number or fraction. The y-intercept is the value of y when $x = 0$ (the point where the line intercepts the y-axis on a graph). Given the slope and y-intercept of a line, the values are substituted for m and b into the equation. A line with a slope of $\frac{1}{2}$ and y-intercept of -2 would have an equation:

$$y = \frac{1}{2}x - 2$$

Example

Q. Xavier was hospitalized with pneumonia. He was originally given 35 mg of antibiotics. Later, after his condition continued to worsen, Xavier's dosage was increased to 60 mg. What was the percent increase of the antibiotics? Round the percentage to the nearest tenth.

   a. 59.4%
   b. 41.7%
   c. 83.6%
   d. 71.4%

Explanation

Answer. D: An increase or decrease in percentage can be calculated by dividing the difference in amounts by the original amount and multiplying by 100. Written as an equation, the formula is:

$$\frac{new\ quantity\ -\ old\ quantity}{old\ quantity} \times 100$$

Here, the question states that the dosage was increased from 35 mg to 60 mg, so these are plugged into the formula to find the percentage increase.

$$\frac{60-35}{35} \times 100 = \frac{25}{35} \times 100$$

$$0.7142 \times 100 = 71.4\%$$

Solve Real-World Situations Using Expressions, Equations, and Inequalities

To translate a word problem into an expression, look for a series of key words indicating addition, subtraction, multiplication, or division:

- Addition: add, altogether, together, plus, increased by, more than, in all, sum, and total
- Subtraction: minus, less than, difference, decreased by, fewer than, remain, and take away
- Multiplication: times, twice, of, double, and triple

Mathematics

- Division: divided by, cut up, half, quotient of, split, and shared equally

By identifying the variables (unknown quantities) in the word problem, you can use the identified operations to create a mathematical expression, equation, or inequality.

Example

Q. Kimberley earns $10 an hour babysitting, and after 10 p.m., she earns $12 an hour. The time she works is rounded to the nearest hour for pay purposes. On her last job, she worked from 5:30 p.m. to 11 p.m. In total, how much did Kimberley earn on her last job?
   a. $45
   b. $57
   c. $62
   d. $42

Explanation

Answer C: Kimberley worked 4.5 hours at the rate of $10/h and 1 hour at the rate of $12/h. The problem states that her time is rounded to the nearest hour, so the 4.5 hours would round up to 5 hours at the rate of $10/h.

$$(5h) \times \left(\frac{\$10}{h}\right) + (1h) \times \left(\frac{\$12}{h}\right) = \$50 + \$12 = \$62$$

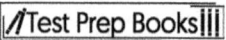

Measurement and Data

Interpret Relevant Information from Tables, Charts, and Graphs

Tables

One of the most common ways to express data is in a **table**. The primary reason for plugging data into a table is to make interpretation more convenient. It's much easier to look at the table than to analyze results in a narrative paragraph. When analyzing a

Mathematics

table, pay close attention to the title, variables, and data.

Results of Antibiotic Studies		
Group	Dosage of Antibiotics in milligrams (mg)	Efficacy (% of participants cured)
A	0 mg	20%
B	20 mg	40%
C	40 mg	75%
D	60 mg	95%
E	80 mg	100%
F	100 mg	100%

Graphs

Graphs provide a visual representation of data. The variables are placed on the two axes. The bottom of the graph is referred to as the horizontal axis or X-axis. The left-hand side of the graph is known as the vertical axis or Y-axis. Typically, the independent variable is placed on the X-axis, and the dependent variable is located on the Y-axis.

The most common types of graphs are the bar graph and the line graph.

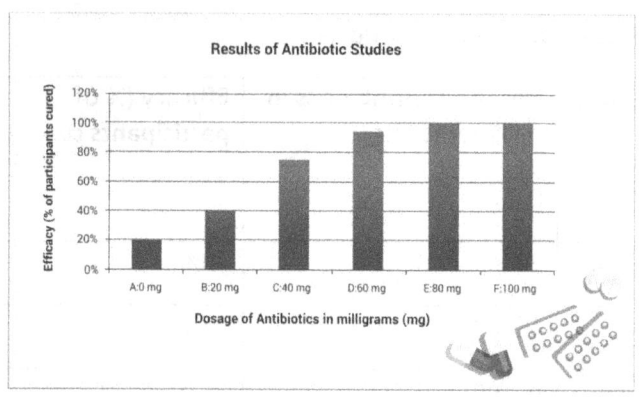

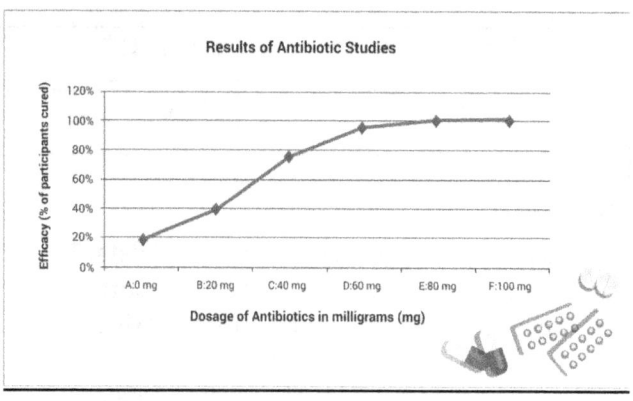

Mathematics

Charts

Chart is a broad term that refers to a variety of ways to represent data.

To graph relations, the **Cartesian plane** is used. This means to think of the plane as being given a grid of squares, with one direction being the x-axis and the other direction the y-axis.

Negative values mean to move left or down; positive values mean to move right or up. The point where the axes cross one another is called the **origin**. The origin has coordinates $(0, 0)$ and is usually called O when given a specific label.

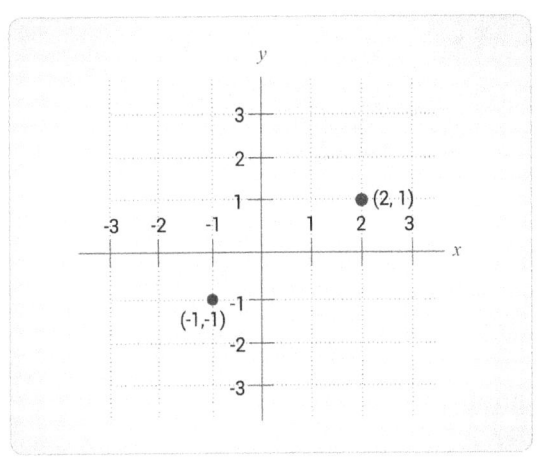

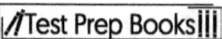 **Mathematics**

Other types of charts include line plots, tally charts, picture graphs, circle graphs/pie charts, scatter plots, and line graphs.

Example

Q. The following graph compares the various test scores of the top three students in each of these teacher's classes. Based on the graph, which teacher's students had the lowest range of test scores?

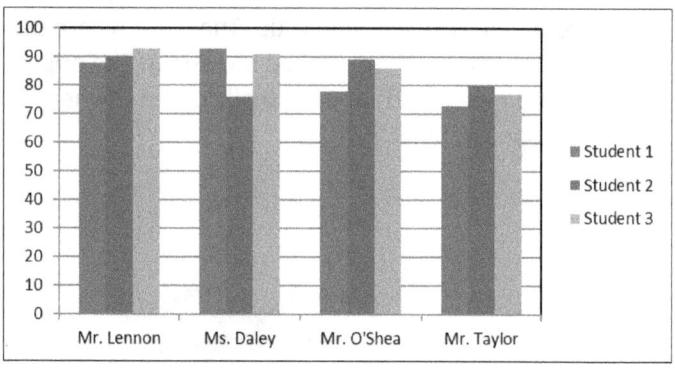

- a. Mr. Lennon
- b. Mr. O'Shea
- c. Mr. Taylor
- d. Ms. Daley

Explanation

Answer. A: To calculate the range in a set of data, subtract the highest value with the lowest value. In this graph, the range of Mr. Lennon's students is 5, which can be seen physically in the graph as having the smallest difference compared with the other teachers between the highest value and the lowest value.

Evaluate the Information in Data Sets, Tables, Charts, and Graphs Using Statistics

Mean, Median, and Mode

The center of a set of data can be represented by its mean, median, or mode. These are sometimes referred to as **measures of central tendency**. The **mean** is the average. To find the mean, add up all the data points, then divide by the total number of data points. In a data set, the **median** is the point in the middle. The middle refers to the point where half the data comes before it and half comes after, when the data is recorded in numerical order. The **mode** is the data point that appears most frequently. If two or more data points all tie for the most frequent appearance, then each of them is considered a mode.

Describe a Set of Data

A **set of data** can be described in terms of its center, spread, shape and any unusual features.

The center of a data set can be measured by its mean, median, or mode. The spread of a data set refers to how far the data points are from the center (mean or median). A data set with all its data points clustered around the center will have a small spread. A data set covering a wide range of values will have a large spread.

To determine the range of a set of data, find the minimum and maximum value of the data points within the set. The range is calculated by subtracting the lowest value from the highest value in the set and expressing the solution as an absolute value.

When a data set is displayed as a graph, the shape indicates if a sample is normally distributed, symmetrical, or has measures of skewness.

A description of a data set should include any unusual features such as gaps or outliers. A gap is a span within the range of the data set containing no data points. An outlier is a data point with a value either extremely large or extremely small when compared to the other values in the set.

Correlation

An ***X-Y* diagram**, also known as a scatter diagram, visually displays the relationship between two variables. The independent variable is placed on the x-axis, and the dependent variable is placed on the y-

Mathematics

axis. An *X-Y* diagram may demonstrate a positive, negative, or no correlation between the two variables.

Calculate Probabilities to Determine the Likelihood of an Outcome

Given a set of possible outcomes X, a probability distribution on X is a function that assigns a probability to each possible outcome. The probability of a given outcome must be between zero and 1, while the total probability must be 1.

Example

Q. What is the overall median of Dwayne's current scores: 78, 92, 83, 97?

    a. 19
    b. 85
    c. 83
    d. 87.5

Explanation

Answer. D: For an even number of total values, the *median* is calculated by finding the *mean,* or average, of the two middle values once all values have been arranged in ascending order from least to greatest. In this case, $(92 + 83) \div 2$ would equal the median 87.5, Choice *D*.

Explain the Relationship Between Two Variables

In an experiment, variables are the key to analyzing data. Variables can represent anything, including objects, conditions, events, and amounts of time. There is usually one variable that is controlled, the independent variable, and one that depends on this variable, the dependent variable. If there is a relationship between the two variables, then they are said to be **correlated**.

Covariance is a general term referring to how two variables move in relation to each other.

Constant variables remain unchanged by the scientist across all trials.

Independent variables are also controlled by the scientist, but they are the same only for each group or trial in the experiment.

Dependent variables experience change caused by the independent variable and are what is being measured or observed.

Mathematics

Example

Q. In testing how quickly a rat dies by the amount of poison it eats, which of the following is the independent variable and which is the dependent variable?

    a. How quickly the rat dies is the independent variable; the amount of poison is the dependent variable.

    b. The amount of poison is the independent variable; how quickly the rat dies is the dependent variable.

    c. Whether the rat eats the poison is the independent variable; how quickly the rat dies is the dependent variable.

    d. The cage the rat is kept in is the independent variable; the amount of poison is the dependent variable.

Explanation

Answer. B: The independent variable is the variable manipulated, and the dependent variable is the result of the changes in the independent variable. Choice *B* is correct because the amount of poison is the variable that is changed, and the speed of rat death is the result of the changes in the amount of poison administered.

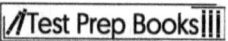
Mathematics

Calculate Geometric Quantities

Perimeter

Length is the measurement of distance from one point to another point, often measured in units of feet, meters, or related units. **Perimeter** is the measurement of a distance around something or the sum of all sides of a polygon. Formulas for measuring perimeters are below.

- Square: $P = 4 \times s$
- Rectangle: $P = l + l + w + w = 2l + 2w$
- Triangle: $P = a + b + c$
- Circle: $\pi \times d$
- Irregular shapes: The perimeter of an irregular polygon is found by adding the lengths of all of the sides. If a side length is missing it must be determined before the perimeter can be calculated.

Area

Area in mathematics is defined as the space occupied by a two-dimensional object. Below are various area formulas.

- Square: $A = s^2$
- Rectangle: $A = l \times w$
- Triangle: $A = \frac{bh}{2}$

Mathematics

- Circle: $A = \pi \times r^2$
- Irregular shapes: The area of an irregular polygon is found by breaking the figure into smaller shapes, finding the area of the smaller shapes, and then adding the areas of the smaller shapes together to produce the total area of the area of the original figure.

Volume

Volume in mathematics is defined as the space occupied by a three-dimensional object. Below are various volume formulas.

Rectangular prism: $V = xyz$
Rectangular pyramid: $V = \frac{1}{3}xyh$
Sphere: $V = \frac{4}{3}\pi r^3$

Surface Area

Surface area in mathematics is defined as the space covering the outside of a three-dimensional object. Below are various surface area formulas.

Rectangular prism: $SA = 2xy + 2yz + 2xz$
Rectangular pyramid: calculate the area of each face of the pyramid and add them together.
Sphere: $A = 4\pi r^2$

Arc

The **arc of a circle** is the distance between two points on the circle. The length of the arc of a circle in terms of degrees is easily determined if the value of the central angle is known. The length of the arc is simply the value of the central angle. In this example, the length of the arc of the circle in degrees is 75°.

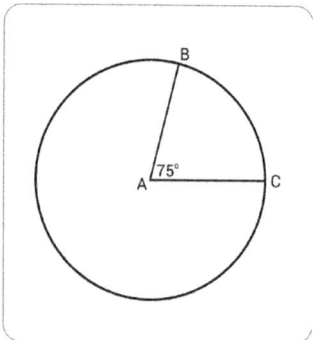

To determine the length of the arc of a circle in distance, the values for both the central angle and the radius must be known. This formula is:

$$\frac{central\ angle}{360°} = \frac{arc\ length}{2\pi r}$$

The equation is simplified by cross-multiplying to solve for the arc length.

Mathematics

Example

Q. The total perimeter of a rectangle is 36 cm. If the length is 12 cm, what is the width?

   a. 3 cm
   b. 12 cm
   c. 6 cm
   d. 8 cm

Explanation

Answer. C: The first step is to substitute all of the data into the formula:

$$36 = 2(12) + 2W$$

Simplify by multiplying 2×12:

$$36 = 24 + 2W$$

Simplifying this further by subtracting 24 on each side, which gives:

$$36 - 24 = 24 - 24 + 2W$$

$$12 = 2W$$

Divide by 2:

$$6 = W$$

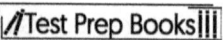

Convert Within and Between Standard and Metric Systems

American Measuring System

The measuring system used today in the United States developed from the British units of measurement during colonial times. The most typically used units in this customary system are those used to measure weight, liquid volume, and length, whose common units are found below.

Common Customary Measurements		
Length	Weight	Capacity
1 foot = 12 inches	1 pound = 16 ounces	1 cup = 8 fluid ounces
1 yard = 3 feet	1 ton = 2,000 pounds	1 pint = 2 cups
1 yard = 36 inches		1 quart = 2 pints
1 mile = 1,760 yards		1 quart = 4 cups
1 mile = 5,280 feet		1 gallon = 4 quarts
		1 gallon = 16 cups

Metric System

Aside from the United States, most countries in the world have adopted the metric system embodied in the International System of Units (SI). The three main

Mathematics

SI base units used in the metric system are the meter (m), the kilogram (kg), and the liter (L); meters measure length, kilograms measure mass, and liters measure volume.

These three units can use different prefixes, which indicate larger or smaller versions of the unit by powers of ten. This can be thought of as making a new unit, which is sized by multiplying the original unit in size by a factor.

These prefixes and associated factors are:

Metric Prefixes			
Prefix	Symbol	Multiplier	Exponential
kilo	k	1,000	10^3
hecto	h	100	10^2
deca	da	10	10^1
no prefix		1	10^0
deci	d	0.1	10^{-1}
centi	c	0.01	10^{-2}
milli	m	0.001	10^{-3}

Conversion

Converting measurements in different units between the two systems can be difficult because they follow different rules. The table below lists some common

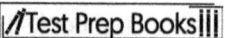 **Mathematics**

conversion values that are useful for problems involving measurements with units in both systems:

English System	Metric System
1 inch	2.54 cm
1 foot	0.3048 m
1 yard	0.914 m
1 mile	1.609 km
1 ounce	28.35 g
1 pound	0.454 kg
1 fluid ounce	29.574 mL
1 quart	0.946 L
1 gallon	3.785 L

Example

Q. Mom's car drove 72 miles in 90 minutes. How fast did she drive in feet per second?

    a. 0.8 feet per second
    b. 48.9 feet per second
    c. 0.009 feet per second
    d. 70.4 feet per second

Explanation

Answer. D: This problem can be solved by using unit conversion. The initial units are miles per minute. The final units need to be feet per second. Converting miles to feet uses the equivalence statement $1 \text{ mi} = 5{,}280 \text{ ft}$. Converting minutes to seconds uses the

Mathematics

equivalence statement 1 min = 60 s. Setting up the ratios to convert the units is shown in the following equation:

$$\frac{72 \text{ mi}}{90 \text{ min}} \times \frac{1 \text{ min}}{60 \text{ s}} \times \frac{5{,}280 \text{ ft}}{1 \text{ mi}} = 70.4 \frac{\text{ft}}{\text{s}}$$

The initial units cancel out, and the new units are left.

Science

Human Anatomy and Physiology

Demonstrate Knowledge of the General Orientation of Human Anatomy

Anatomy may be defined as the structural makeup of an organism. **Physiology** refers to the functions of an organism, and it examines the chemical or physical functions that help the body function appropriately.

<u>Body Cavities</u>
The body is partitioned into different hollow spaces that house organs. The human body contains the following **cavities**:

- Cranial cavity: surrounded by the skull and contains organs such as the brain and pituitary gland.

- Thoracic cavity: encircled by the sternum (breastbone) and ribs and contains organs such as the lungs, heart, trachea (windpipe), esophagus, and bronchial tubes.

- Abdominal cavity: separated from the thoracic cavity by the diaphragm and contains organs such as the stomach, gallbladder, liver, small intestines, and large intestines.

- Pelvic cavity: enclosed by the pelvis, or bones of the hip. It contains organs such as the urinary bladder, urethra, ureters, anus, rectum, and reproductive organs.

- Spinal cavity: surrounded by the vertebral column. The spinal cord runs through the middle of the spinal cavity.

Three Primary Body Planes

A plane is an imaginary flat surface. The three primary planes of the human body are coronal (frontal), sagittal (longitudinal), and transverse (axial).

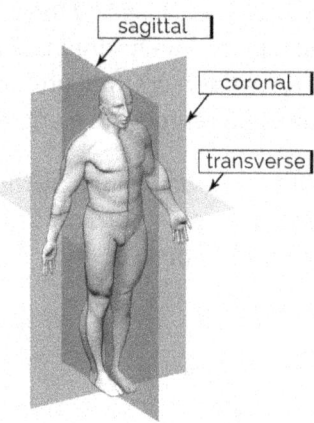

Terms of Direction

- **Medial** refers to a structure being closer to the midline of the body.
- **Lateral** refers to a structure being farther from the midline of the body.
- **Proximal** refers to a structure or body part located near an attachment point.
- **Distal** refers to a structure or body part located far from an attachment point.

- **Anterior (ventral)** means toward the front in humans.
- **Posterior (dorsal)** means toward the back in humans.
- **Superior (cephalic/cranial)** means above and refers to a structure closer to the head.
- **Inferior (caudal)** means below and refers to a structure farther from the head.
- **Superficial** refers to a structure closer to the surface.
- **Deep** refers to a structure farther from the surface.

Body Regions

- Terms for general locations on the body include:
- Cervical: relating to the neck (can also refer to the cervix, as in cervical cancer)
- Clavicular: relating to the clavicle
- Ocular: relating to the eyes
- Acromial: relating to the shoulder
- Cubital: relating to the elbow
- Brachial: relating to the arm
- Carpal: relating to the wrist
- Thoracic: relating to the chest
- Abdominal: relating to the abdomen
- Pubic: relating to the groin
- Pelvic: relating to the pelvis

- Femoral: relating to the femur, or thigh bone
- Geniculate: relating to the knee
- Pedal: relating to the foot
- Palmar: relating to the palm of the hand
- Plantar: relating to the sole of the foot

Abdominopelvic Regions and Quadrants

The **abdominopelvic region** may be defined as the combination of the abdominal and the pelvic cavities. The region's upper border is the breasts and its lower border is the groin region.

A simple way to describe the abdominopelvic area is to divide it into the following quadrants:

1. **Right upper quadrant (RUQ)**: Encompasses the right hypochondriac, right lumbar, epigastric, and umbilical regions.
2. **Right lower quadrant (RLQ)**: Encompasses the right lumbar, right inguinal, hypogastric, and umbilical regions.
3. **Left upper quadrant (LUQ)**: Encompasses the left hypochondriac, left lumbar, epigastric, and umbilical regions.
4. **Left lower quadrant (LLQ)**: Encompasses the left lumbar, left inguinal, hypogastric, and umbilical regions.

Using a more complex system, the abdominopelvic region can be divided into the following nine sections:

1. **Right hypochondriac**: region below the cartilage of the ribs
2. **Epigastric**: region above the stomach between the hypochondriac regions
3. **Left hypochondriac**: region below the cartilage of the ribs
4. **Right lumbar**: region of the waist
5. **Umbilical**: region between the lumbar regions where the umbilicus, or belly button (navel), is located
6. **Left lumbar**: region of the waist
7. **Right inguinal**: region of the groin
8. **Hypogastric**: region below the stomach between the inguinal regions
9. **Left inguinal**: region of the groin

Levels of Organization of the Human Body

All the parts of the human body are built of individual units called **cells**. Groups of similar cells are arranged into **tissues**, different tissues are arranged into **organs**, and organs working together form entire **organ systems**. The human body has twelve organ systems that govern circulation, digestion, immunity, hormones, movement, support, coordination, urination & excretion, reproduction (male and female), respiration, and general protection.

Example

Q. Using anatomical terms, what is the relationship of the sternum relative to the deltoid?
   a. Medial
   b. Lateral
   c. Superficial
   d. Posterior

Explanation

Answer. A: The sternum is medial to the deltoid because it is much closer to (typically right on) the midline of the body, while the deltoid is lateral at the shoulder cap. Superficial means that a structure is closer to the body surface and posterior means that it falls behind something else. For example, skin is superficial to bone and the kidneys are posterior to the rectus abdominis.

Describe the Anatomy and Physiology of the Respiratory System

The respiratory system enables breathing and supports the energy-making process in cells by transporting an essential reactant, oxygen, to cells so that they can produce energy in their mitochondria via cellular respiration. The respiratory system also removes carbon dioxide, a waste product of cellular respiration.

Science

This system is divided into the upper respiratory system and the lower respiratory system. The upper respiratory system comprises the nose, the nasal cavity and sinuses, and the pharynx. The lower respiratory system comprises the larynx (voice box), the trachea (windpipe), the small passageways leading to the lungs, and the lungs.

A flat muscle underneath the lungs called the diaphragm controls breathing. While breathing can be voluntary, it is mostly under control of the autonomic nervous system.

Functions of the Respiratory System

The most important respiratory function is gas exchange between the air and the circulating blood. It protects the delicate respiratory surfaces from environmental variations and defends them against pathogens. It is responsible for producing the sounds that the body makes for speaking and singing, as well as for non-verbal communication. It also helps regulate blood volume, blood pressure, and blood pH.

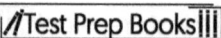
Science

Example

Q. Which of the following is NOT a major function of the respiratory system in humans?

    a. It provides a large surface area for gas exchange of oxygen and carbon dioxide.

    b. It helps regulate the blood's pH.

    c. It helps cushion the heart against jarring motions.

    d. It is responsible for vocalization.

Explanation

Answer. C: Although the lungs may provide some cushioning for the heart when the body is violently struck, this is not a major function of the respiratory system.

Describe the Anatomy and Physiology of the Cardiovascular System

The cardiovascular system (also called the circulatory system) is a network of organs and tubes that transport blood, hormones, nutrients, oxygen, and other gases to cells and tissues throughout the body. The major components of the circulatory system are the blood vessels, blood, and heart.

Blood Vessels

In the circulatory system, blood vessels are responsible for transporting blood throughout the body. The three major types of blood vessels in the circulatory system are **arteries**, **veins**, and **capillaries**. Arteries carry blood from the heart to the rest of the body. Veins carry blood from the body back to the heart. Capillaries connect arteries to veins and form networks that exchange materials between the blood and the cells.

Blood

Blood is vital to the human body. It is a liquid connective tissue that serves as a transport system for supplying cells with nutrients and carrying away their wastes. There are three major types of blood cells: red blood cells (erythrocytes), white blood cells (leukocytes), and platelets.

Heart

The heart is a two-part, muscular pump that forcefully pushes blood throughout the human body. The human heart has four chambers—two upper atria (left and right) and two lower ventricles (left and right) separated by a partition called the septum.

Four valves section off the chambers from one another. The tricuspid valve and mitral valve are the atrioventricular (AV) valves and keep blood from backflowing from the ventricles to the atria. The pulmonary valve and the aortic valve are the semilunar (SL) valves and control blood flow into the pulmonary artery and aorta.

Cardiac Cycle

A cardiac cycle is one complete sequence of cardiac activity. The two phases are **diastole** (when the heart relaxes and fills with blood) and **systole** (when the heart contracts and discharges blood).

Types of Circulation

Five major blood vessels manage blood flow to and from the heart: the superior vena cava and inferior vena cava, the aorta, the pulmonary artery, and the pulmonary vein.

In the human body, there are two types of circulation: pulmonary circulation and systemic circulation. Pulmonary circulation supplies blood to the lungs. Systemic circulation supplies blood to all other parts of the body.

Science

Example

Q. Identify the aorta by placing an "X" on its location:

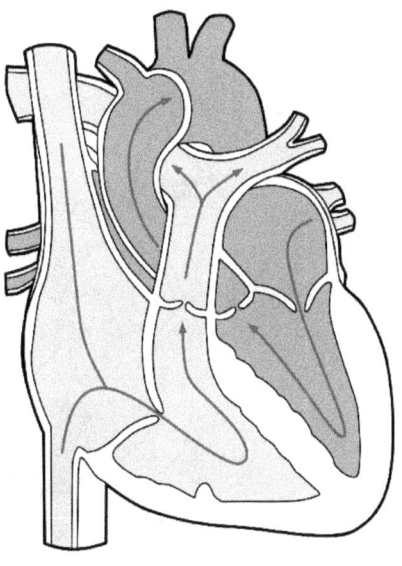

Explanation
Answer. The aorta leads directly from the left ventricle and to the systemic circuit:

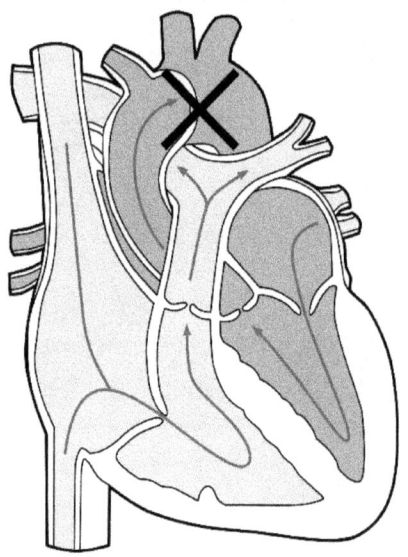

Describe the Anatomy and Physiology of the Digestive System

The human body relies completely on the digestive system to meet its nutritional needs. After food and drink are ingested, the digestive system breaks them down into their component nutrients and absorbs them so that the circulatory system can transport

Science

them to other cells to use for growth, energy, and cell repair. These nutrients may be classified as proteins, lipids, carbohydrates, vitamins, and minerals.

The digestive system has two parts: the digestive tract (also called the alimentary tract or gastrointestinal tract) and the accessory digestive organs. The digestive tract is the pathway in which food is ingested, digested, absorbed, and excreted. It is composed of the mouth, pharynx, esophagus, stomach, small and large intestines, rectum, and anus. **Peristalsis**, or wave-like contractions of smooth muscle, moves food and wastes through the digestive tract. The accessory digestive organs are the salivary glands, liver, gallbladder, and pancreas.

Example

Q. Which locations in the digestive system are sites of chemical digestion?

      I. Mouth
      II. Stomach
      III. Small Intestine

a. II only
b. III only
c. II and III only
d. I, II, and III

Explanation

Answer. D: Chemical digestion involves chemically changing the food and breaking it down into small organic compounds that can be utilized by the cell to build molecules. The salivary glands in the mouth secrete amylase that breaks down starch, which begins chemical digestion. The stomach contains enzymes such as pepsinogen/pepsin and gastric lipase, which chemically digest protein and fats. The small intestine continues to digest protein using the enzymes trypsin and chymotrypsin

Describe the Anatomy and Physiology of the Nervous System

The human nervous system coordinates the body's response to stimuli from inside and outside the body. There are two major types of nervous system cells: neurons and neuroglia. Neurons are the workhorses of the nervous system and form a complex communication network that transmits electrical impulses termed action potentials, while neuroglia connect and support the neurons.

There are two major divisions of the nervous system, central and peripheral. The **central nervous system (CNS)** consists of the brain and spinal cord. Three layers of membranes called the meninges cover and separate the CNS from the rest of the body. The major

Science

divisions of the brain are the forebrain, the midbrain, and the hindbrain.

The **peripheral nervous system (PNS)** includes all nervous tissue besides the brain and spinal cord. The PNS consists of the sets of cranial and spinal nerves and relays information between the CNS and the rest of the body. The PNS has two divisions: the autonomic nervous system and the somatic nervous system. The **autonomic nervous system (ANS)** governs involuntary, or reflexive, body functions. The **somatic nervous system (SNS)** governs the conscious, or voluntary, control of skeletal muscles and their corresponding body movements.

Example
Q. How many neurons generally make up a sensory pathway?
- a. 1
- b. 2
- c. 3
- d. 4

Explanation
Answer. C: Generally, all sensory pathways that extend from the sensory receptor to the brain are composed of three long neurons called the primary, secondary, and tertiary neurons. The primary one stretches from the sensory receptor to the dorsal root

ganglion of the spinal nerve, and the secondary one stretches from the cell body of the primary neuron to the spinal cord or the brain stem. The tertiary one stretches from the cell body of the secondary one into the thalamus.

Describe the Anatomy and Physiology of the Muscular System

The **muscular system** is responsible for involuntary and voluntary movement of the body. There are three types of muscle: skeletal, cardiac, and smooth.

Skeletal muscles, or voluntary muscles, are attached to bones by tendons and are responsible for voluntary movement.

Smooth muscles are responsible for involuntary movement, such as food moving through the digestive tract and blood moving through vessels.

Cardiac muscle cells are found only in the heart, where they control the heart's rhythm and blood pressure.

Example

Q. Which of the following correctly lists the four properties that all types of muscle tissue share?
Select all that apply
- a. Contractile
- b. Excitable
- c. Elastic
- d. Extensible
- e. Voluntary

Explanation

Answer. A, B, C, & D: All three types of muscle tissue (skeletal, cardiac, and smooth) share four important properties: They are contractile, meaning they can shorten and pull on connective tissue; excitable, meaning they respond to stimuli; elastic, meaning they rebound to their original length after a contraction; and extensible, meaning they can be stretched repeatedly but maintain the ability to contract. While skeletal muscle is under voluntary control, both cardiac and smooth muscle are involuntary.

Describe the Anatomy and Physiology of the Male and Female Reproductive System

The reproductive system is responsible for producing, storing, nourishing, and transporting functional reproductive cells, or gametes, in the human body. It includes the reproductive organs, also known as **gonads**, the reproductive tract, the accessory glands and organs that secrete fluids into the reproductive tract, and the perineal structures, which are the external genitalia.

Male Reproductive System

The entire male reproductive system is designed to generate sperm and produce semen that facilitate fertilization of eggs, the female gametes. The **testes** are the endocrine glands that secrete testosterone, a hormone that is important for secondary sex characteristics and sperm development, or **spermatogenesis**. The testes also produce and store 500 million **spermatocytes**, or sperm, which are the male gametes, each day. Testes are housed in the scrotum, which is a sac that hangs outside the body so that spermatogenesis occurs at cooler and optimal conditions.

The sperm, along with various exocrine secretions, are collectively called semen. For sexual intercourse to successfully transfer sperm from the male to the female's egg, the penis must be erect, which occurs via arousal and increased circulation. During sexual intercourse, ejaculation expels the contents of the semen up through the vagina and delivers the sperm to the egg.

Female Reproductive System

The vagina is the passageway that sperm must travel through to reach an egg, the female gamete. Surrounding the vagina are the labia minor and labia major, both of which are folds that protect the urethra, which is used for urination and is part of the urinary system, and the vaginal opening. The clitoris is above the vagina and urethra.

The female gonads are the ovaries. After puberty, ovaries generally alternate producing one egg per month, which is then delivered to the uterus via the fallopian tubes. Ovaries also secrete the hormones estrogen and progesterone. The 28-day average journey of the egg to the uterus is called the **menstrual cycle**, and it is highly regulated by the endocrine system and a variety of hormones.

Fertilization can only happen around **ovulation**, when the egg is inside the fallopian tube. The resulting zygote, or fertilized egg, travels down the tube and implants into the uterine wall. The uterus protects and nourishes the developing embryo for nine months, until it is ready for the outside environment. After birth, mammary glands, or breasts, produce milk to feed the baby.

If the egg released is unfertilized, the uterine lining will slough off during menstruation.

Example

Q. Which of the following creates sperm?
   a. Prostate gland
   b. Seminal vesicles
   c. Scrotum
   d. Seminiferous tubules

Explanation

Answer. D: The seminiferous tubules are responsible for sperm production. Had *testicles* been an answer choice, it would also have been correct since it houses the seminiferous tubules. The prostate gland (*A*) secretes enzymes that help nourish sperm after creation. The seminal vesicles (*B*) secrete some of the components of semen. The scrotum (*C)* is the pouch holding the testicles.

Describe the Anatomy and Physiology of the Integumentary System

The integumentary system includes skin, hair, nails, oil glands, and sweat glands. The largest organ of the integumentary system (and of the body), the skin, acts as a barrier and protects the body from mechanical impact, variations in temperature, microorganisms, chemicals, and UV radiation from the sun. It regulates body temperature, peripheral circulation, and excretes waste through sweat. It also contains a large network of nerve cells that relay changes in the external environment to the brain.

Skin consists of three layers, the surface epidermis, the inner dermis, and the subcutaneous hypodermis. Sweat glands and sebaceous glands, or oil glands, are important exocrine glands found in the skin. The three major functions of skin are protection, regulation, and sensation.

Example
Q. Which of the following areas of the body has the most sweat glands?
    a. Upper back
    b. Arms
    c. Feet
    d. Palms

Explanation
Answer. A: The upper back has one of the highest densities of sweat glands of any area on the body.

Describe the Anatomy and Physiology of the Endocrine System

The endocrine system is made up of the ductless tissues and glands that secrete hormones directly into the bloodstream. It is similar to the nervous system in that it controls various functions of the body, but it does so via secretion of hormones in the bloodstream as opposed to nerve impulses. The endocrine system is also different because its effects last longer than that of the nervous system. Nerve impulses are immediate while hormone responses can last for minutes or even days.

The endocrine system works closely with the nervous system to regulate the physiological activities of the other systems of the body in order to maintain homeostasis. Hormone secretions are controlled by tight feedback loops that are generally regulated by the hypothalamus, the bridge between the nervous and endocrine systems.

Hormones are chemicals that bind to specific target cells. There are two types of hormones: steroid and protein.

The major endocrine glands are:

> 1. **Hypothalamus**: part of the brain. Connects the nervous system to the endocrine system.
> 2. **Pituitary gland**: regulates other endocrine glands.
> 3. **Thymus gland**: produces several hormones that are important for development and maintenance of T lymphocytes, which are important for immunity.

4. **Adrenal gland**: produces epinephrine and norepinephrine which cause the "fight or flight" response in the face of danger or stress.

5. **Pineal gland**: secretes the hormone melatonin, which regulates the body's circadian rhythm, which governs the natural wake-sleep cycle.

6. **Testes and ovaries**: secrete testosterone and both estrogen and progesterone, respectively. They are responsible for secondary sex characteristics, gamete development, and female hormones are important for embryonic development.

7. **Thyroid gland**: releases hormones like thyroxine, which regulates metabolism, and calcitonin, which lowers calcium levels in the body.

8. **Parathyroid glands**: secrete parathyroid hormone (PTH), which increases calcium levels in the body.

9. **Pancreas**: regulates blood sugar levels by secreting insulin to lower them or glucagon to raise them.

Example

Q. The primary function of the endocrine system is to maintain which of the following?

a. Heartbeat
b. Respiration
c. Electrolyte and water balance
d. Homeostasis

Explanation

Answer. D: The primary function of the endocrine system is to maintain homeostasis, which means it makes constant adjustments to the body's systemic physiology to maintain a stable internal environment.

Describe the Anatomy and Physiology of the Urinary System

The urinary system is made up of the kidneys, ureters, urinary bladder, and the urethra. It is the system responsible for removing waste products and balancing water and electrolyte concentrations in the blood. The urinary system has many important functions related to waste excretion. It regulates the concentrations of sodium, potassium, chloride, calcium, and other ions in the filtrate by controlling the amount of each that is reabsorbed during filtration. It also regulates blood pH, blood volume, blood pressure, and red blood cell production. Kidney

Science

cells also synthesize calcitriol, which is a hormone derivative of vitamin D3 that aids in calcium ion absorption by the intestinal epithelium.

Example

Q. Which of the following are functions of the urinary system?

> I. Synthesizing calcitriol and secreting erythropoietin
> II. Regulating the concentrations of sodium, potassium, chloride, calcium, and other ions
> III. Reabsorbing or secreting hydrogen ions and bicarbonate
> IV. Detecting reductions in blood volume and pressure

a. I, II, and III
b. II and III
c. II, III, and IV
d. All of the above

Explanation

Answer. D: The urinary system has many functions, the primary of which is removing waste products and balancing water and electrolyte concentrations in the blood. It also plays a key role in regulating ion concentrations, such as sodium, potassium, chloride, and calcium, in the filtrate. The urinary system helps maintain blood pH by reabsorbing or secreting hydrogen ions and bicarbonate as necessary. Certain kidney cells can detect reductions in blood volume and pressure and then can secrete renin to activate a hormone that causes increased reabsorption of sodium ions and water.

Describe the Anatomy and Physiology of the Immune System

The immune system is the body's defense against invading microorganisms (bacteria, viruses, fungi, and parasites) and other harmful, foreign substances. It is capable of limiting or preventing infection.

There are two general types of immunity: innate immunity and acquired immunity. **Innate immunity** uses physical and chemical barriers to block microorganism entry into the body. **Acquired immunity** refers to a specific set of events used by the body to fight a particular infection. Essentially, the body accumulates and stores information about the nature of an invading microorganism.

Acquired immunity is divided into a primary response and a secondary response. The **primary immune response** occurs the first time a particular microorganism enters the body. The **secondary immune response** takes place during subsequent encounters with a known microorganism.

Science

The **lymphatic system** includes the spleen, thymus, tonsils, lymph nodes, lymphatic vessels, and the lymph. The main function of the lymphatic system is protection against infection. The system also conserves body fluids and proteins and absorbs vitamins from the digestive system.

Example

Q. Which is the first event to happen in a primary immune response?

    a. Macrophages ingest pathogens and present their antigens.
    b. Neutrophils aggregate and act as cytotoxic, nonspecific killers of pathogens.
    c. B lymphocytes make pathogen-specific antibodies.
    d. Helper T cells secrete interleukins to activate pathogen-fighting cells.

Explanation

Answer. A: The first event that happens in a primary immune response is that macrophages ingest pathogens and display their antigens. Then, they secrete interleukin 1 to recruit helper T cells. Once helper T cells are activated, they secrete interleukin 2 to stimulate plasma B and killer T cell production. Only then can plasma B make the pathogen specific antibodies.

Describe the Anatomy and Physiology of the Skeletal System

The skeletal system is composed of 206 bones interconnected by tough connective tissue called ligaments. The axial skeleton can be considered the north-south axis of the skeleton. It includes the spinal column, sternum, ribs, and skull. There are eighty bones in the axial skeleton, and thirty-three of them are vertebrae. The ribs make up twelve of the bones in the axial skeleton.

The remaining 126 bones are in the **appendicular skeleton**, which contains bones of the appendages like the collarbone (clavicle), shoulders (scapula), arms, hands, hips, legs, and feet.

One of the skeletal system's most important functions is to protect vital internal organs. Additionally, the organization of the skeleton allows us to stand upright and acts as a foundation for organs and tissues to attach and maintain their location. Moreover, the skeletal system and the muscular system are physically interconnected and allow for voluntary movement.

Example

Q. What makes bone resistant to shattering?
　a. The calcium salts deposited in the bone
　b. The collagen fibers
　c. The bone marrow and network of blood vessels
　d. The intricate balance of minerals and collagen fibers

Explanation

Answer. D: Bone matrix is an intricate lattice of collagen fibers and mineral salts, particularly calcium and phosphorus. The mineral salts are strong but brittle, and the collagen fibers are weak but flexible, so the combination of the two makes bone resistant to shattering and able to withstand the normal forces applied to it.

Biology

Describe Cell Structure, Function, and Organization

Cell Structure and Function

The **cell** is the main functional and structural component of all living organisms. The cell theory is composed of three principals:

1. All organisms are composed of cells.
2. All existing cells are created from other living cells.
3. The cell is the most fundamental unit of life.

Organisms can be unicellular (composed of one cell) or multicellular (composed of many cells). All cells must be bounded by a cell membrane, be filled with cytoplasm of some sort, and be coded by a genetic sequence.

Prokaryotes and Eukaryotes

Prokaryotic cells are much smaller than **eukaryotic cells**. The majority of prokaryotes are unicellular, while the majority of eukaryotes are multicellular. The majority of prokaryotic cells have cell walls, while most eukaryotic cells do not have cell walls. The DNA of prokaryotic cells is contained in a single circular chromosome in an area called the nucleoid, while the DNA of eukaryotic cells is contained in multiple linear chromosomes in the nucleus. Prokaryotic cells divide using binary fission, while eukaryotic cells divide using mitosis. Examples of prokaryotes are bacteria and archaea while examples of eukaryotes are animals and plants.

Nuclear Parts of a Cell

- **Nucleus**: Houses a cell's genetic material, deoxyribonucleic acid (DNA)
- **Chromosomes**: Complex thread-like arrangements composed of DNA found in a cell's nucleus.
- **Chromatin**: An aggregate of genetic material consisting of DNA and proteins called histones that forms chromosomes during cell division.
- **Histones**: Octameric (eight-part) proteins that enable condensing of DNA.
- **Nucleolus**: The largest component of the nucleus of a eukaryotic cell.

Cell Membranes

Cell membranes encircle the cell's cytoplasm, separating the intracellular environment from the extracellular environment. They are selectively permeable, which enables them to control molecular traffic entering and exiting cells.

Active Transport Mechanisms

Active transport refers to the energy-requiring migration of molecules across a cell membrane. It's a useful way to move molecules from an area of low concentration to an area of high concentration. Adenosine triphosphate (ATP), the currency of cellular energy, is needed to work against the concentration gradient. **Endocytosis** and **exocytosis** are two examples of active transport.

Passive Transport Mechanisms

Passive transport refers to the migration of molecules across a cell membrane that does not require energy. The three types of passive transport are simple diffusion, facilitated diffusion, and osmosis.

Simple diffusion relies on a concentration gradient, or differing quantities of molecules inside or outside of a cell. **Facilitated diffusion** utilizes carrier proteins to transport molecules across a cell membrane. **Osmosis** refers to the transport of water across a selectively permeable membrane.

Structure and Function of Cellular Organelles

Organelles are specialized structures that perform specific tasks in a cell. The term literally means "little organ." Most organelles are membrane bound and serve as sites for the production or degradation of chemicals.

Science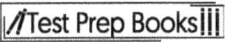

You can view an illustration of the cell and some common organelles by using the link or QR code:

testprepbooks.com/bonus/teas7pocket

Cell Cycle

Mitosis is the process of cell division and replication in which the cell (mother) copies itself to produce two genetically identical daughter cells. **Meiosis** is the process of cell division in which the cell (mother) produces four cells with half of the mother cell's original genetic information. This is the process by which gametes (sperm and eggs) are formed.

Cellular Respiration

Cellular respiration is the catabolic process of breaking down the bonds in glucose and releasing its potential energy in the form of ATP, or adenosine triphosphate. ATP harnesses small amounts of energy and uses it for processes in cellular metabolism. Each glucose molecule can produce about 32 ATP molecules. Breaking glucose and storing its energy in smaller molecules enables the cells to distribute energy across many metabolic reactions instead of just one.

Example

Q. Which is the cellular organelle used for digestion to recycle materials?

    a. The Golgi apparatus
    b. The lysosome
    c. The centrioles
    d. The mitochondria

Explanation

Answer. B: The cell structure responsible for cellular storage, digestion, and waste removal is the lysosome. Lysosomes are like recycle bins. They are filled with digestive enzymes that facilitate catabolic reactions to regenerate monomers. The Golgi apparatus is designed to tag, package, and ship out proteins destined for other cells or locations. The centrioles typically play a large role only in cell division when they ratchet the chromosomes from the mitotic plate to the poles of the cell. The mitochondria are involved in energy production and are the powerhouses of the cell.

Describe the Relationship Between Genetic Material and the Structure of Proteins

Chromosome Structure

A chromosome is a condensed form of deoxyribonucleic acid (DNA) that consists of two sister chromatids joined by a centromere. A chromatid is a duplicated chromosome that has not separated. Under an electron micrograph, a chromosome appears as short X-shaped bar-like rods composed of condensed coiled chromatin threads. Chromatin is DNA wrapped around histone proteins and appears as bumpy threads under a light microscope. The bumps are nucleosomes, flat disc-shaped clusters of eight histone proteins. DNA wraps around the nucleosome twice and is connected to another cluster via a DNA segment or linker. The histone proteins package very long strands of DNA in an ordered manner and have a role in gene regulation.

Nucleic Acids

Nucleotides are monomers that link together to form nucleic acids. Nucleotides have three components: a nitrogenous base (purine and pyrimidine) and a phosphate functional group both attached to a five-carbon sugar (deoxyribose and ribose). The two types of purines are guanine (G) and adenine (A), while the three types of pyrimidines are thymine (T), cytosine

(C), and uracil (U). Nucleotides containing deoxyribose are termed deoxyribonucleic acids (DNA) and utilize guanine, adenine, cytosine, and thymine as their nitrogen bases. Nucleotides containing ribose are termed ribonucleic acids (RNA) and utilize guanine, adenine, cytosine, and uracil as their nitrogenous bases.

Codons

A codon represents a sequence of three nucleotides that codes for either one specific amino acid or a stop signal during protein synthesis. Codons are found on messenger RNA (mRNA). The full set of codons encompasses 64 possible combinations and is termed the **genetic code**.

RNA

Ribonucleic acid (RNA) plays crucial roles in protein synthesis and gene regulation. RNA is made of nucleotides consisting of ribose (a sugar), a phosphate group, and one of four possible nitrogenous bases—adenine (A), cytosine (C), guanine (G), and uracil (U). RNA utilizes the nitrogenous base uracil in place of the base thymine found in DNA. Another difference between RNA and DNA is that RNA is typically found as a single-stranded structure, while DNA typically exists in a double-stranded structure. RNA can be categorized into three major groups—messenger RNA

Science

(mRNA), ribosomal RNA (rRNA), and transfer RNA (tRNA).

DNA

Deoxyribonucleic acid, or DNA, contains the genetic material that is passed from parents to offspring. It contains specific instructions for the development and function of a unique eukaryotic organism. The vast majority of cells in any eukaryotic organism contains the same DNA. The structure of DNA visually approximates a twisting ladder, and is described as a double helix. DNA is made of nucleotides consisting of deoxyribose (a sugar), a phosphate group, and one of four possible nitrogenous bases—thymine (T), adenine (A), cytosine (C), and guanine (G). The sequence of these bases dictates the instructions contained in the DNA, making each species singular. Weak hydrogen bonds between the nitrogenous bases ensures easy uncoiling of DNA's double helical structure in preparation for replication.

Transcription

Transcription refers to a portion of DNA being copied into RNA, specifically mRNA. It is the first crucial step in gene expression.

Translation

Translation refers to the process of ribosomes synthesizing proteins. It represents the second crucial step in gene expression. The instructions encoding specific proteins to be made are contained in codons on mRNA, which have previously been transcribed from DNA. Each codon represents a specific amino acid or stop signal in the genetic code.

DNA Replication

During DNA replication, identical copies of the cell's genome are passed to the two formed daughter cells. Replication occurs on the chromatin threads. Because of the DNA molecule's length, replications occur at several origin points along the chain. There are four sequences of events during the replication of DNA: uncoiling, separation, assembly, and restoration.

Genetic Mutations

Mutations occur when single DNA base-pairs are altered or when an improper codon is added to the chain.

Example

Q. Which of the following is directly transcribed from DNA and represents the first step in protein building?
    a. siRNA
    b. rRNA
    c. mRNA
    d. tRNA

Explanation

Answer. C: mRNA is directly transcribed from DNA before being taken to the cytoplasm and translated by rRNA into a protein. tRNA transfers amino acids from the cytoplasm to the rRNA for use in building these proteins. siRNA is a special type of RNA which interferes with other strands of mRNA, typically by causing them to get degraded by the cell rather than translated into protein.

Apply Concepts Underlying Mendel's Laws of Inheritance

Genes are the basis of heredity. The German scientist Gregor Mendel first suggested the existence of genes in 1866. A gene can be pinpointed to a **locus**, or a particular position, on DNA. It is estimated that humans have approximately 20,000 to 25,000 genes. For any particular gene, a human inherits one copy from each parent for a total of two.

Genotype refers to the genetic makeup of an individual within a species. **Phenotype** refers to the visible characteristics and observable behavior of an individual within a species. The genetic material (DNA) inherited from an individual's parents determines the genotype. Natural selection leads to adaptations within a species, which affects the phenotype.

Genotypes are written with pairs of letters that represent alleles. Alleles are different versions of the same gene, and, in simple systems, each gene has one dominant allele and one recessive allele. **Homozygous** means that the individual inherits two alleles of the same type, while **heterozygous** means inheriting one dominant allele and one recessive allele. Recessive alleles are only expressed when two recessive alleles are inherited.

Mendel's Laws of Genetics and Punnett Squares

Mendel's first law of genetics is the principle of **segregation** and states that alleles will segregate into different cells during the formation of gametes in meiosis. Mendel's second law of genetics is the principle of **independent assortment** and states that genes for different traits will be assigned to different gametes independent of the others. Together, these two laws state the assumptions upon which genetic probabilities are based.

Punnett squares are simple graphic representations of all the possible genotypes of offspring, given the genotypes of the parent organisms.

For example, in a species of bird with black or white feathers, *A* represents a dominant allele and determines white colored feathers on a bird. The recessive allele *a* determines black colored feathers on a bird. If both parents are heterozygous (*Aa*, the x and y-axis of the Punnett square below), the offspring will have the possible genotypes *AA, Aa, Aa*, and *aa*. Phenotypically, three offspring would have white feathers and one would have black feathers:

	A	a
A	AA (White)	Aa (White)
a	Aa (White)	Aa (Black)

Example

Q. What information does a genotype give that a phenotype does not?

    a. The genotype necessarily includes the proteins coded for by its alleles.

    b. The genotype will always show an organism's recessive alleles.

    c. The genotype must include the organism's physical characteristics.

    d. The genotype shows what an organism's parents looked like.

Explanation

Answer. B: Since the genotype is a depiction of the specific alleles that an organism's genes code for, it includes recessive genes that may or may not be otherwise expressed.

Describe Structure and Function of the Basic Macromolecules in a Biological System

There are four classes of macromolecules that allow organisms to exist: carbohydrates, lipids, proteins, and nucleic acids.

Carbohydrates

Carbohydrates are sweet, ring-like sugar molecules that are built from carbon (carbo-), oxygen, and hydrogen (-hydrates, meaning water). They can exist as one-ring monosaccharides, like glucose, fructose, and galactose, or as two-ring disaccharides, like lactose, maltose, and sucrose. These simple sugars can be easily broken down and used via glycolysis to provide a source of quick energy. Polysaccharides are repeating chains of monosaccharide rings. They are more complex carbohydrates, and there are several types including starch, glycogen, cellulose, and chitin.

Proteins

Proteins are composed of chains of amino acids. There are twenty amino acids that can be combined to make different proteins. The varying amino acids are linked by peptide bonds and form the primary structure of the polypeptide, or chain of amino acids. The primary structure is just the string of amino acids. It is the secondary, tertiary, and quaternary structure that determines protein shape and function.

Proteins are synthesized through **translation**.

Lipids

Lipids are mostly nonpolar, hydrophobic molecules that are not soluble in water. Lipids consist of triglycerides, phospholipids, and steroids.

Triglycerides consist of fats (solids) or oils (liquid) that are produced by the addition of a single glycerol molecule to three fatty acid chains. These energy-storage molecules can exist as saturated fats or unsaturated fats.

Phospholipids are composed of glycerol, two fatty acid tails, and a hydrophilic phosphate group. The amphipathic nature of this molecule results in a lipid bilayer where the "water-loving" hydrophilic heads face the extracellular matrix and cytoplasm and the "water-hating" hydrophobic tails face each other on the inside.

Steroids are another type of lipid. Cholesterol is a steroid that is embedded in animal cell membranes and acts as a fluidity buffer. Steroid hormones such as testosterone and estrogen are responsible for transcriptional regulation in certain cells.

Nucleic Acids

Nucleic acids have two important duties in the body. As monomers, they are crucial for energy transfer. As polymers, they are a fundamental component of genetic material, as discussed above. Monomers form the building blocks of macromolecules, while polymers are formed when monomers link together in chains, forming larger macromolecules.

Science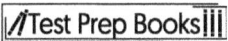

Example

Q. Which of the following correctly matches a category of protein with a physiologic example?
   a. Keratin is a structural protein.
   b. Antigens are hormonal proteins.
   c. Channel proteins are marker proteins.
   d. Actin is a transport protein.

Explanation

Answer. A: Keratin is a structural protein and it is the primary constituent of things like hair and nails.

Describe the Role of Micro-Organisms in Disease

Microorganisms are tiny single-celled or multicellular organisms that can only be seen through a microscope. Microorganisms have an important role in the environment, as they're found all over and help to recycle nutrients and energy. Four main classes of microorganisms are viruses, bacteria, protozoa, and fungi.

Viruses are acellular, using a host species to replicate themselves, allowing for the cycling of nutrients, bacteria, and algae. They can also be pathogens and spread diseases.

Bacteria are unicellular and obtain energy through photosynthesis, chemosynthesis, and heterotropism. The domain *Bacteria* includes many of the prokaryotic species that people encounter daily. While many bacteria are beneficial, some are parasitic, meaning they live within a host and cause disease.

Protozoa are a diverse group of unicellular organisms that carry out complex metabolic activities. They're non-photosynthetic, so they cannot use light as an energy source. Amoebae, flagellates, and ciliates are all protozoa.

Fungi can be unicellular or multicellular and they convert organic matter into nutrients. Fungi includes yeasts, molds, and mushrooms. They are the primary decomposers of an ecological system.

Infectious Diseases and Prevention

Infectious diseases are caused by the spread of microorganisms from one person to another, either directly or indirectly. It is important to be able to control microorganisms to prevent the transmission and spread of diseases, and to stop decomposition of organisms and food spoilage. They can be controlled by both physical and chemical methods. **Physical control** can occur through changes in temperature, humidity, osmotic pressure, and by filtration. **Chemical control** occurs using disinfectants,

Science

antibiotics, antiseptics, and antimicrobial chemicals, which all work by selective toxicity (seeking out and killing the microorganisms without harming anything else).

Example

Q. Which of the following is NOT an example of a chemical control method of disease prevention?
 a. Disinfectant spray
 b. Antibacterial ointment
 c. Dehumidifier
 d. Antimalarial medication

Explanation

Answer. C: A dehumidifier removes excess water from the air, which can help prevent the growth of toxic fungi such as black mold. Disinfectant sprays, antibacterial ointments, and antimalarial medications are all examples of chemical controls, making them incorrect answers.

Chemistry

Recognize Basic Atomic Structure

Measurable Properties of Atoms

All matter is made of atoms. An **atom** is the most basic component of an element that still retains its properties. The structure of an atom has two major components: the atomic nucleus and the atomic shells (also known as orbitals). The nucleus is found in the center of an atom. The three major subatomic particles are protons, neutrons, and electrons and are found in the atomic nucleus and shells.

Protons, Neutrons, and Electrons

Protons are found in the atomic nucleus and are positively charged particles. The addition or removal of protons from an atom's nucleus creates an entirely different element. **Neutrons** are also found in the atomic nucleus and are neutral particles, meaning they have no net electrical charge. The addition or removal of neutrons from an atom's nucleus does not create a different element but instead creates a lighter or heavier form of that element called an isotope. **Electrons** are found orbiting in the atomic shells around the nucleus and are negatively charged particles. A proton or a neutron has nearly 2,000 times the mass of an electron.

Electrons and Chemical Bonds

Electrons orbit the nucleus in atomic shells, or electron clouds, each of which can accommodate a certain number of electrons. For example, the first atomic shell can accommodate two electrons, the second atomic shell can hold a maximum of eight electrons, and the third atomic shell can house a maximum of eight electrons.

Chemical bonding typically results in the formation of a new substance, called a compound. Only the electrons in the outermost atomic shell are able to form chemical bonds. These electrons are known as valence electrons, and they are what determines the chemical properties of an atom.

Periodicity and the Periodic Table

All of the elements known to man are catalogued in the **periodic table**, a chart of elements arranged by increasing atomic number. The **atomic number** refers to the number of protons in an atom's nucleus. An **isotope** is a variation of an element having the same number of protons, but a different number of neutrons.

Periodicity refers to the repeating patterns, or trends, in the properties of elements. The atomic number and atomic structure are the key determinants of the properties of elements.

The **periodic table** catalogues all of the elements known to man, currently 118, arranged in order of increasing atomic number. It is one of the most important references in the science of chemistry. Information that can be gathered from the periodic table includes the element's atomic number, atomic mass, and chemical symbol.

It is also arranged in horizontal rows known as **periods**, and vertical columns known as **families**, or **groups**. Elements in the periodic table can also be classified into three major groups: metals, metalloids, and nonmetals. Metals are concentrated on the left side of the periodic table, while nonmetals are found on the right side. Metalloids occupy the area between the metals and nonmetals.

Trends in the properties of elements in the periodic table include electron configurations, atomic radius, electronegativity, ionization energy, and electron affinity. As the atomic number increases, electrons gradually fill the shells of an atom. In general, the start of a new period corresponds to the first time an electron inhabits a new shell. Moving left to right in a period, trends reveal decreasing atomic radius, increasing electronegativity, increasing ionization energy, and increasing electron affinity. Moving from top to bottom in a group, trends reveal increasing

Science

atomic radius, decreasing electronegativity, and decreasing ionization energy.

You can view a periodic table by using the link or QR code:

testprepbooks.com/bonus/teas7pocket

Science

Example

Q. The following elements all are found on the right side of the periodic table, in the p-block:

1. Fluorine (F)
2. Oxygen (O)
3. Neon (NE)
4. Tin (Sn)

List them from least reactive to most reactive below:

1. _____

2. _____

3. _____

4. _____

Explanation

Answer.

1. Neon
2. Tin
3. Oxygen
4. Fluorine

Neon, one of the noble gases, is chemically inert or not reactive because it contains eight valence electrons in the outermost shell. The atomic number is 10, with a 2.8 electron arrangement, meaning that there are 2 electrons in the inner shell and the remaining 8 electrons in the outer shell. This is extremely stable for the atom, so it will not want to add or subtract any of its electrons and will not react under typical circumstances. In contrast, fluorine is the most reactive halogen owing to its high electronegativity, so it is placed at the bottom. Oxygen is slightly less reactive, possessing a lower affinity for electrons, while tin, a post-transition metal, is relatively unreactive (although not inert like neon), placing them at #3 and #2 respectively.

Physical Properties and Changes of Matter

States of Matter—Liquids, Gases, and Solids

There are three fundamental states of matter—liquid, gas, and solid.

Liquid

The molecules in a **liquid** are not in an orderly arrangement and can move past one another. Weak intermolecular forces contribute to a liquid having an indefinite shape, but definite volume. Lastly, a liquid conforms to the shape of its container, is not easily compressible, and flows quite easily.

Gas

The molecules in a **gas** have a large amount of space between them. A gas will diffuse indefinitely if unconfined, while it will assume the shape and volume of its container if enclosed. In other words, a gas has no definite shape or volume. Lastly, a gas is compressible and flows quite easily.

Solid

The molecules in a **solid** are closely packed together, which restricts their movement. Very strong intermolecular forces contribute to a solid having a definite shape and volume. Furthermore, a solid is not easily compressible and does not flow easily.

Phase Transitions

States of matter are able to undergo phase transitions, or changes. Phase changes are best described in terms of temperature and kinetic energy.

If enough heat is added to a solid, the particles will move quickly enough that they will begin to slide past each other and form a liquid. Moving from a solid to a liquid is called **melting**. The opposite change is **freezing**. Freezing occurs when liquid particles move slower and pack closely together into a solid.

Moving from a liquid to a gas due to increased kinetic energy is called **vaporization**. There are two types of

Science

vaporization—evaporation and boiling. **Evaporation** is a surface phenomenon and involves the conversion of a liquid into a gas below the boiling temperature at a given pressure. **Boiling** occurs below the surface and involves the conversion of liquid into a gas at or above the boiling temperature. The opposite reaction is **condensation**, which occurs when gas particles slow down and form a liquid.

Less common are direct changes from either solid to gas, or **sublimation**, or from a gas to a solid, or **deposition**.

The physical properties of matter do not change the chemical composition of a substance.

Example
Q. Which of the following is a chief difference between evaporation and boiling?
   a. Liquids boil only at the surface, while they evaporate equally throughout the liquid.
   b. Evaporating substances change from gas to liquid, while boiling substances change from liquid to gas.
   c. Evaporation happens in nature, while boiling is a manmade phenomenon.
   d. Evaporation can happen below a liquid's boiling point.

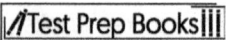

Explanation

Answer. D: Evaporation takes place at the surface of a fluid, while boiling takes place throughout the fluid. The liquid will boil when it reaches its boiling or vaporization temperature, but evaporation can happen due to a liquid's volatility. Volatile substances often coexist as a liquid and as a gas, depending on the pressure forced on them. The phase change from gas to liquid is condensation, and both evaporation and boiling take place in nature.

Describe Chemical Reactions

Valence Electrons

Valence electrons are found on the outermost shell of an atom. Atoms containing valence electrons are involved in chemical reactions, and elements with similar valence-shell configurations have similar chemical properties within a group in the periodic table.

Chemical Bonds Between Atoms

Chemical bonds refer to the manner in which atoms are attached to one another. Atoms may be held together with three fundamental types of chemical bonds—ionic, covalent, or hydrogen.

Ionic bonds are formed from the electrostatic attractions between oppositely charged atoms. In an ionic bond, an atom loses one or more electrons to another atom which gains them. The atoms do this so that they can achieve a full outermost shell of electrons, which is the configuration that is most stable, and these are typically the strongest types of bonds.

Due to their very strong bonding, ionic compounds have several distinct characteristics. They have high melting points, high boiling points, and are brittle and crystalline. They are arranged in rigid, well-defined structures, which allows them to break apart along smooth, flat planes.

Covalent bonds are formed when two atoms share electrons, instead of transferring them like in ionic compounds. The atoms in covalent compounds have a balance of attraction and repulsion between their protons and electrons, which keeps them bonded together. Two atoms can be joined by single, double, or triple covalent bonds.

Covalent substances have low melting and boiling points and are also poor conductors of heat and electricity. Covalent bonds are the most plentiful type of bond making up the human body and are a crucial source of energy for living organisms. Covalent bonds are comparable in strength to ionic bonds, but stronger than hydrogen bonds, and are typically used to bind the basic macromolecules—carbohydrates, lipids, nucleic acids, and proteins—together.

Hydrogen bonds are temporary and weak. They typically occur between two partial, opposite electrical charges. For example, hydrogen bonds form when a hydrogen (H) atom is in the vicinity of nitrogen (N), fluorine (F), or oxygen (O) atoms. These partial electrical charges are called **dipoles** and are caused by the unequal sharing of electrons between covalent bonds. Water is the most prevalent molecule that forms hydrogen bonds; these bonds contribute to the adhesiveness and cohesiveness properties of water.

Metallic bonds are formed by electrons that move freely through a metal. They are the product of the force of attraction between electrons and metal ions. The electrons are shared by many metal ions and act like glue holding the metallic substance together.

Metallic compounds have characteristic properties including strength, conduction of heat and electricity, and malleability. They can conduct electricity by passing energy through the freely moving electrons, creating a current. These compounds also have high melting and boiling points.

Types of Chemical Reactions

Chemical reactions are characterized by a chemical change in which the starting substances, or **reactants**, differ from the substances formed, or **products**. Chemical reactions may involve a change in color, the production of gas, the formation of a precipitate, or changes in heat content. The following are the basic types of chemical reactions:

- **Decomposition**: A compound is broken down into two or more smaller elements or compounds.

- **Synthesis**: Two or more elements or compounds are joined together.

- **Single Displacement**: A single element or ion takes the place of another in a compound.

- **Double Displacement**: Two elements or ions exchange a single atom each to form two different compounds.

- **Oxidation-Reduction**: Elements undergo a change in oxidation number. Also known as a **redox reaction**.

- **Acid-Base**: Involves a reaction between an acid and a base, usually producing a salt and water.

- **Combustion**: A hydrocarbon (a compound composed of only hydrogen and carbon) reacts with oxygen to form carbon dioxide and water.

Balancing Chemical Reactions

Chemical reactions are expressed using chemical equations. Chemical equations must be balanced with equivalent numbers of atoms for each type of element on each side of the equation based on the **Law of Conservation of Mass**. The reactants are located on the left side of the arrow, while the products are located on the right side of the arrow. Coefficients are the numbers in front of the chemical formulas. Subscripts are the numbers to the lower right of chemical symbols in a formula. To tally atoms, one should multiply the formula's coefficient by the subscript of each chemical symbol. For example, the chemical equation $2 H_2 + O_2 \rightarrow 2H_2O$ is balanced.

Example

Q. Salts like sodium iodide (NaI) and potassium chloride (KCl) use what type of bond?

    a. Ionic bonds
    b. Disulfide bridges
    c. Covalent bonds
    d. London dispersion forces

Explanation
Answer. A: Salts are formed from compounds that use ionic bonds.

Demonstrate How Conditions Affect Chemical Reactions

Factors that Affect the Rate of a Reaction

There are a variety of factors that affect the rate of a reaction, such as temperature, surface area of the reactants, and a variety of environmental factors. Reaction concentration is another major factor, except in zero-order processes. In a **zero-order process**, the reaction rate does not depend on the concentration of the reactants and is equal to the rate constant: $reaction\ rate = k$. In **nonzero order processes**, the rate will depend on many factors. A **catalyst** is a chemical substance or enzyme that allows the rate of reaction to increase without being consumed and lowers the activation energy needed to form a product.

Introduction to Equilibrium

Many chemical reactions are **reversible**, which means that the reactants can form the products, or the products can react to form the reactants. Depending on the environmental and experimental conditions, the reaction can be driven in either direction.

Chemical reactions reach a state of **equilibrium** when the rate of the forward reaction is equivalent to the rate of the reverse reaction. The concentrations of the reactants and products are proportional to each other with regard to the stoichiometry of the equation and are no longer changing at equilibrium.

Reaction Quotient and Equilibrium Constant

The **reactant quotient**, **Q**, measures the proportions of the reactants and products at any given point in the reaction, not just at equilibrium. The value of Q gives a picture of the progression of the reaction. As its value approaches that of the **equilibrium constant**, **K**, the reaction gets closer to an equilibrium state. When $Q = K$, equilibrium is reached.

Introduction to Le Chatelier's Principle

Le Chatelier's principle is a law of equilibrium that states that if a system at equilibrium is subjected to a change in the environment, the system will react accordingly to counter the change and restore its state of equilibrium. Disruptions to the system can include changes to the temperature, volume, or pressure of a gas, or the concentration of any of the reactants or products.

Introduction to Solubility Equilibria

When a salt substance is dissolved in a solvent, it is considered a reversible reaction because the substance can be precipitated out of the solvent again. The reaction quotient, Q, of the reaction describes the concentration of the reactants and products at any time of the reaction. The equilibrium constant for solubility reactions is K_{sp}. The value of K_{sp} is dependent on the solubility of the salt in the solvent. Large K_{sp} values indicate greater dissociation of the salt molecule and greater solubility.

Catalysts

Catalysts are substances that accelerate the speed of a chemical reaction. A catalyst remains unchanged throughout the course of a chemical reaction. Catalysts increase the rate of a chemical reaction by providing an alternate path requiring less activation energy. Activation energy refers to the amount of energy required for the initiation of a chemical reaction.

Enzymes

Enzymes are a class of catalysts instrumental in biochemical reactions. Like all catalysts, enzymes increase the rate of a chemical reaction by providing an alternate path requiring less activation energy. Enzymes are proteins and possess an active site, which is the part of the molecule that binds the reacting molecule, or substrate. The "lock and key" analogy is used to describe the substrate key fitting precisely into the active site of the enzyme lock to form an enzyme-substrate complex.

Example
Q. Most catalysts found in biological systems are which of the following?
 a. Special lipids called cofactors
 b. Special proteins called enzymes
 c. Special lipids called enzymes
 d. Special proteins called cofactors

Explanation
Answer. B: Biological catalysts are termed *enzymes*, which are proteins with conformations that specifically manipulate reactants into positions which decrease the reaction's activation energy.

Understand Properties of Solutions

Explaining Characteristic Properties of Substances
Properties of Water
Water is the most abundant molecule on Earth. It is a compound composed of hydrogen and oxygen with the chemical formula H_2O. Water is also **polar**, which means it is negatively charged at one end and positively charged at the other end. The oxygen is more **electronegative** than the hydrogens, meaning

that its protons pull in more of the electrons than the hydrogens. This leaves the oxygen with a partial negative charge and the hydrogens with a partial positive charge. Water is **amphoteric** and **self-ionizable**. No other substance on Earth may be found naturally in all three states of matter—liquid, solid, and gas. Water is also unique due to its liquid state being denser than its solid state (ice), which is why ice floats in liquid water. Water is considered the universal solvent because it can dissolve many substances. Many of the properties of water are due to its polarity and hydrogen bonding. Water has the following properties:

- Cohesiveness
- Adhesiveness
- High specific heat
- High surface tension
- High heat of vaporization

Properties of Molecules

Molecules have both physical and chemical properties. Physical properties describe a substance in isolation, while chemical properties describe how a substance reacts with others.

There are two types of physical properties: extensive and intensive. **Extensive physical properties** depend on the amount of a substance. Volume, length, and mass are all examples of extensive properties. **Intensive physical properties** are static and unchanging properties of a substance that identify it. Extensive properties are important for measurement and recording data but do not identify a substance. Intensive properties are critical for identification.

Physical changes do not change the intensive physical properties of a substance. Chemical changes, on the other hand, transform substances so that they have new physical properties. While physical properties describe the characteristics of a substance, chemical like properties describe how it **behaves** in chemical reactions.

Solutions and Mixtures

A **solution** is a homogenous mixture of more than one substance. A **solute** is another substance that can be dissolved into a substance called a **solvent.** If only a small amount of solute is dissolved in a solvent, the solution formed is said to be **diluted**. A solution is considered **concentrated** if a large amount of solute is dissolved into the solvent. If more solute is being added to a solvent, but not dissolving, the solution is called **saturated.** This level, at which a solvent cannot accept and dissolve any more solute, is called its **saturation point**. In some cases, it is possible to force more solute to be dissolved into a solvent, but this will result in crystallization. The state of a solution on the verge of crystallization, or in the process of crystallization, is called a **supersaturated** solution.

All parts of a solution are identical. Solutions can be solids, liquids, or gases. In a liquid solution, the solute that is dissolved into the solvent can be a solid, liquid, or gas. Because of their homogeneous composition, solutions cannot be separated by filtration. They also cannot scatter visible light.

The method for calculating the concentration of a solution is done through finding its molarity. The **molality** of a solution, abbreviated as m, is defined as the moles of solute dissolved in one kilogram of solvent. More commonly, solutions are described in terms of **molarity**, abbreviated as M, which describes the number of moles of solute dissolved per liter of solution. In some instances, such as environmental reporting, molarity is measured in **parts per million** (ppm). Parts per million is the number of milligrams of a substance dissolved in one liter of water.

Example

Q. Which of the following is a special property of water?

    a. Water easily flows through phospholipid bilayers.

    b. A water molecule's oxygen atom allows fish to breathe.

    c. Water is highly cohesive which explains its high boiling point.

    d. Water can self-hydrolyze and decompose into hydrogen and oxygen.

Explanation

Answer. C: Water's polarity lends it to be extremely cohesive and adhesive; this cohesion keeps its atoms very close together. Because of this, it takes a large amount of energy to boil its liquid form.

Science

Describe Concepts of Acids and Bases

pH refers to the power or potential of hydrogen atoms and is used as a scale for a substance's acidity. The pH scale is a logarithmic scale used to quantify how acidic or basic a substance is. The pH scale typically ranges from zero to 14, although it is possible to have pHs outside of this range. Pure water has a pH of 7, which is considered neutral. pH values less than 7 are considered acidic, while pH values greater than 7 are considered basic, or alkaline:

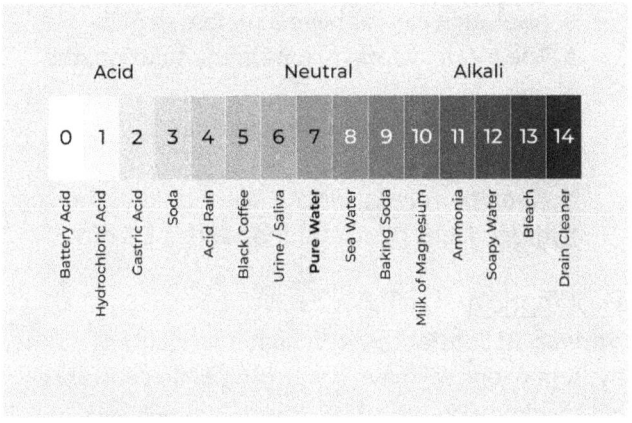

Generally speaking, an acid is a substance capable of donating hydrogen ions, while a base is a substance capable of accepting hydrogen ions. A buffer is a molecule that can act as either a hydrogen ion donor or acceptor. Buffers are crucial in the blood and body fluids, and prevent the body's pH from fluctuating into dangerous territory.

The combination of an acid with a base produces water and an ionic compound (a salt) in a process referred to as a neutralization reaction. Whether the salt is soluble or insoluble in water depends on the reactants.

Example

Q. Which statement is true about the pH of a solution?

    a. A solution cannot have a pH less than 1.
    b. The more hydroxide ions in the solution, the higher the pH.
    c. If an acid has a pH of greater than 2, it is considered a weak base.
    d. A solution with a pH of 2 has ten times more hydrogen ions than a solution with a pH of 1.

Explanation

Answer. B: Substances with higher amounts of hydrogen ions will have lower pHs, while substances with higher amounts of hydroxide ions will have higher pHs. Choice *A* is incorrect because it is possible to have an extremely strong acid with a pH less than 1, as long as its molarity of hydrogen ions is greater than 1. Choice *C* is false because a weak base is determined by having a pH lower than some value, not higher.

Substances with pHs greater than 2 include anything from neutral water to extremely caustic lye. Choice *D* is false because a solution with a pH of 2 has ten times fewer hydrogen ions than a solution of pH 1.

Scientific Reasoning

Use Basic Scientific Measurements and Measurement Tools

Technology is always advancing, and its application is playing an increasingly larger role in science research. Technology increases the accuracy and precision of scientific data, which in many ways is becoming more dependent on the type of technology adopted.

Mathematics has been around for centuries and has constantly been called upon in scientific research to help understand and explain the workings of the natural world. It is a crucial part of the scientific method. Mathematics can help improve and refine the asking of questions or hypotheses in a scientific argument.

Units

When recording data, it is of the utmost importance to also record units. Acceptable customary units in the U.S. include feet, gallons, and pounds, which measure length, volume, and mass, respectively. Laboratory data is typically recorded with SI units which are universally used. Standard SI units include the following:

- Second (s) for time
- Meter (m) for length
- Gram (g) for mass
- Liter (L) for volume
- Celsius (°C) or Kelvin (K) for temperature (°C + 273 = K)

Prefixes such as nano, micro, milli, kilo, mega, giga, etc., also indicate the scale of SI measurements.

Scientific Notation, Rounding, and Significant Figures

Scientific notation should be used when appropriate. The correct form is to have the ones unit followed by the decimal point with the appropriate number of significant figures followed by an indication of the power of ten.

For example: $1{,}320{,}000 = 1.32 \times 10^6$

Science

Rounding should be used to the correct number of significant figures. 0-4 always keeps the preceding number as is while 5-9 raises it.

For example: 1.325 rounds to 1.33
4.289 rounds to 4.29

Significant figures should be used, meaning that measurements too precise to be recorded should not be included. Significant figures have a few rules. Any non-zero number preceding a decimal point is significant and any trailing zeros are not significant. Zeroes between numbers are always significant. After the decimal point, any preceding zeroes are not significant while any trailing zeroes are.

For example: 3,570,000 has 3 significant figures.
0.000008320 has 4 significant figures.

Scale

Different situations call for different units of measurement, or different scales. It is important to be mindful of scale, especially when working in medicine. Larger weights can be measured in kilograms or pounds; however, these units are inappropriate units for very small objects. Temperature has three different scales: Kelvin, Celsius, and Fahrenheit.

Example

Q. Which of the following correctly displays 8,600,000,000,000 in scientific notation (to two significant figures)?

    a. 8.6×10^{12}
    b. 8.6×10^{-12}
    c. 8.6×10^{11}
    d. 8.60×10^{12}

Explanation

Answer. A: The decimal point for this value is located after the final zero. Because the decimal is moved 12 places to the left in order to get it between the *8* and the *6*, then the resulting exponent is positive, so Choice *A* is the correct answer. Choice *B* is false because the decimal has been moved in the wrong direction. Choice *C* is incorrect because the decimal has been moved an incorrect number of times. Choice *D* is false because this value is written to three significant figures, not two.

$$8,\underbrace{6}_{12}\underbrace{0}_{11}\underbrace{0}_{10},\underbrace{0}_{9}\underbrace{0}_{8}\underbrace{0}_{7},\underbrace{0}_{6}\underbrace{0}_{5}\underbrace{0}_{4},\underbrace{0}_{3}\underbrace{0}_{2}\underbrace{0}_{1}$$

Apply Logic and Evidence to a Scientific Explanation

A scientific explanation has three crucial components—a claim, evidence, and logical reasoning. A **claim** makes an assertion or conclusion focusing on the original question or problem. The **evidence** provides backing for the claim and is usually in the form of scientific data. The scientific data must be appropriate and sufficient. The scientific **reasoning** connects the claim and evidence and explains why the evidence supports the claim.

Scientific explanations have two fundamental characteristics. First, they should explain all scientific data and observations gleaned from experiments. Second, they should allow for predictions that can be verified with future experiments.

It's important to focus on the **empirical**, or observable/tangible evidence, in an experiment. Doing so helps remove a researcher's personal **bias** towards what they think or hope to be true.

Example

Q. A researcher is exploring factors that contribute to the GPA of college students. While the sample is small, the researcher is trying to determine what the data shows. What can be reasoned from the table below?

Student	Maintains a Calendar?	Takes Notes?	GPA
A	sometimes	often	3.1
B	never	always	3.9
C	never	never	2.0
D	sometimes	often	2.7

a. No college students consistently maintain a calendar of events.

b. There is an inverse correlation between maintaining a calendar and GPA, and there is a positive correlation between taking notes and GPA.

c. There is a positive correlation between maintaining a calendar and GPA, and there is no correlation between taking notes and GPA.

d. There is no correlation between maintaining a calendar and GPA, and there is a positive correlation between taking notes and GPA.

Explanation

Answer. D: Based on this table, it can be reasoned that there is not a correlation between maintaining a calendar and GPA, since Student B never maintains a calendar but has the highest GPA of the cohort. Furthermore, it can be reasoned that there is a positive correlation between taking notes and GPA since the more notes a student takes, the higher the GPA they have. Thus, Choice D is the correct answer. Choice A offers an absolute that cannot be proven based on this study; thus, it is incorrect. Choices B and C are incorrect because they have at least one incorrect correlation.

Predict Relationships Among Events, Objects, and Processes

Cause and Effect

The cause is *why* something happens, and the effect is *what* actually happens.

While it is typical for there to be a single cause and a single effect in a relationship, there are many situations that call for a cause to have many effects, such as exploring the effects of a certain event. In exploring the effects of exercise, for example, the cause is exercise. Effects are stress relief, increased energy, and weight loss.

There is the possibility that one effect can have many causes. For example, type 2 diabetes is not a one-cause disease, but rather a combination of exercise habits, diet, and genetics.

Unit Size
In understanding relationships between objects encountered in science, it's important to understand the scale of them. This is accomplished by understanding the size of different units of measurement.

Example
Q. Jackson wants to open a dog-training business. He wants to see which dog treat is most effective in training dogs to sit. If he wants to design an experiment testing twenty dogs to figure out which treats to use, what would be a good dependent variable?

    a. Type of food
    b. Time in seconds the dogs sit
    c. How many times the dog wags its tail
    d. Shape of food

Explanation
Answer. B: Time in seconds the dogs sit. This is a better choice than Choice *C* (tail wagging) because it is a measurable, meaningful, and relevant dependent variable. Tail wagging, although quantitative, is not a

valid measure of anything. Choices *A* and *D* could be independent variables in the experiment.

Apply the Scientific Method to Interpret a Scientific Investigation

The scientific method provides the framework for studying and learning about the world in a scientific fashion. There is no consensus as to the number of steps involved in executing the scientific method, but the following six steps are needed to fulfill the criteria for correct usage of the scientific method:

- Ask a question
- Make observations
- Create or propose a hypothesis
- Formulate an experiment
- Test the hypothesis
- Accept or reject the hypothesis

Example

Q. A student believes that there is an inverse relationship between sugar consumption and test scores. To test this hypothesis, he recruits several people to eat sugar, wait one hour, and take a short aptitude test afterwards. The student will compile the participants' sugar intake levels and test scores. How should the student conduct the experiment?

    a. One round of testing, where each participant consumes a different level of sugar.
    b. Two rounds of testing: The first, where each participant consumes a different level of sugar, and the second, where each participant consumes the same level as they did in Round 1.
    c. Two rounds of testing: The first, where each participant consumes the same level of sugar as each other, and the second, where each participant consumes the same level of sugar as each other but at higher levels than in Round 1.
    d. One round of testing, where each participant consumes the same level of sugar.

Explanation

Answer. C: To gather accurate data, the student must be able compare a participant's test score from round 1 with their test score from round 2. The differing levels of intellect among the participants means that comparing participants' test scores to those of other participants would be inaccurate.

English and Language Usage

Conventions of Standard English

Standard English Spelling

Misspellings reduce a writer's credibility and can create misunderstandings. Keep these spelling guidelines in mind, remembering there are often exceptions in the English language:

1. Each syllable must have at least one vowel.

2. A short vowel sound indicates only one vowel is needed, such as in *cat* or *red*. If the word has a long vowel sound, add another vowel, either alongside it or separated by a consonant: bed/*bead*; mad/*made*. When the second vowel is separated by two consonants— *madder*—it does not affect the first vowel's sound.

3. Although there are exceptions, remember the saying, "*I* before *e* except after *c* or when sounding as *a* as in *neighbor* or *weigh*."

4. When two vowels are next to each other, the first one makes the sound, and the second one is silent. An example is the word *beam*.

Homophones
Homophones are two or more words that have no particular relationship to one another except their identical pronunciations (do, due, dew).

Irregular Plurals
Irregular plurals are words that aren't made plural the usual way, by adding *–s* (book/books, day/days). Irregular plurals follow different rules such as: church/churches, baby/babies, potato/potatoes, wolf/wolves, deer/deer, man/men, mouse/mice, goose/geese, foot/feet.

Contractions
To make **contractions,** combine two words by inserting an apostrophe (') in the space where a letter is omitted. For example, to combine *you* and *are*, drop the *a* and put the apostrophe in its place: *you're*.

Note that *it's*, when spelled with an apostrophe, is always the contraction for *it is*. The possessive form of the word is written without an apostrophe as *its*.

Capitalization

Here's a non-exhaustive list of things that should be capitalized:

1. The first word of every sentence
2. The first word of every line of poetry
3. The first letter of proper nouns (World War II)
4. Holidays (Valentine's Day)
5. The days of the week and months of the year (Tuesday, March)
6. The first word, last word, and all major words in the titles of books, movies, songs, and other creative works (In the novel, *To Kill a Mockingbird,* note that *a* is lowercase since it's not a major word, but *to* is capitalized since it's the first word of the title.)
7. Titles when preceding a proper noun (President Roberto Gonzales, Aunt Judy)

When simply using a word such as *president* or *secretary*, though, the title is not capitalized.

> Officers of the new business must include a *president* and *treasurer*.

Seasons—spring, fall, etc.—are not capitalized.

North, *south*, *east*, and *west* are capitalized when referring to regions but are not when being used for directions. In general, if it's preceded by *the* it should be capitalized.

> I'm from the South.
> I drove south.

Example

Q. Which of the following uses correct spelling?
a. Leslie knew that training for the Philadelphia Marathon would take dicsipline and perserverance, but she was up to the challenge.
b. Leslie knew that training for the Philadelphia Marathon would take discipline and perseverence, but she was up to the challenge.
c. Leslie knew that training for the Philadelphia Marathon would take disiplin and perservearance, but she was up to the challenge.
d. Leslie knew that training for the Philadelphia Marathon would take discipline and perseverance, but she was up to the challenge.

Explanation

Answer. D: *Discipline* and *perseverance* are both spelled correctly in Choice *D*. These are both considered commonly misspelled words. One or both words are spelled incorrectly in choices A, B, and C.

Conventions of Standard English Punctuation

Ellipses

An **ellipsis** consists of three dots (...) that indicate a word or phrase has been left out of the writing material. Writers will use them to save space or to focus only on the specifically relevant material. The ellipsis may also be used to show a pause in sentence flow.

Commas

A **comma** (,) is a punctuation mark that has several different purposes such as setting apart a word or a phrase in a sentence, connecting sentences, or separating items in lists. Here is a list of comma usage:

- In a complex sentence, if a subordinate clause comes before the main clause, a comma is placed after the subordinate clause: "After the game was over, we went to the best restaurant in town."

- Two commas are used on either side of an interrupting word or phrase: "Our teacher, Mrs. Dowlen, taught us how to use a compass."

English and Language Usage

- An introductory or interrupting phrase at the beginning of a sentence: "While feeding her puppy, Heather realized he also needed water."

- A comma should go after an interjection or a transitional phrase:

    > "Oh yes, I love that movie."
    > "Also, it is not possible."

- Two commas are used on either side of an abbreviation: "Barry Potter, M.D., specializes in heart disorders."

- Two commas are used on either side of direct addresses: "Yes, Claudia, I am tired and going to bed."

- A comma should be used to list three or more items in a sequence: "My favorite foods are lobster, corn, and potatoes."

- When expressing a date, commas should go after the month and day, preceding the year. If there is a day of the week, commas should follow that as well, before expressing the date: "My birthday was on Tuesday, March 19, 2016."

- Place a comma in between a city and a state: "My parents live in Louisville, KY."

Semicolons

The **semicolon** (;) is a punctuation mark with a couple of different uses:

- A semicolon separates two independent clauses: "I will walk to school; I will not take the bus."

- The semicolon separates a list of items that already contains a comma: "Last summer we travelled to Austin, Texas; Boise, Idaho; and Little Rock, Arkansas."

Colons

Colons (:) have a few different uses:

- Colons can be used to introduce a list after an independent clause: "I brought the following drinks: iced tea, lemonade, and water."

- Colons are used to introduce appositives: "The family got what they needed: a reliable vehicle."

- While a comma is more common, a colon can also precede a formal quotation: "He said to the crowd: 'Let's begin!'"

English and Language Usage

- Colons can also be used after the greeting in a formal letter: "Dear Madam:"

- Colons are used in the writing of time and of ratios:

    "The clock says 12:30 pm."
    "The ratio of mice to men is 50:1."

Hyphens

The **hyphen** is a small dash mark (-) used to link words together. Let's look at a few uses below:

- Hyphens are used to create compound adjectives: "free-range eggs."

- Some words are built with hyphens, such as "merry-go-round," or "well-being."

- Hyphens always go after certain prefixes: "anti-" and "all-."

Parentheses and Dashes

Parentheses () set off a word, phrase, or sentence that is an afterthought, explanation, or side note relevant to the surrounding text but not essential.

An **en-dash** (–) is used to mean "through" by marking a set of dates or a set of numbers, like 1930–1950, or 1–10. It is also used behind affixes.

The **em-dash** (—) is used to set apart relevant but not necessary words or phrases inside of a text. It is longer than a hyphen (-) and an en-dash (–). Using em-dashes sets phrases apart, but unlike commas or parentheses, draws more attention to the aside: "Despite rampant coulrophobia—an irrational fear of clowns—Bobo still books more parties and receives higher rates of compensation per show."

Quotation Marks
Quotation marks (" ") have several uses.

- Quotation marks are used by authors to create dialogue: Henry replied, "The horses have come back."

- Quotation marks are used around short stories, titles of poems, titles of songs, essays, and book chapters: "The Tell-Tale Heart," "The Road Not Taken," "Piano Man," "Why I Write," "I: Elementary Rules of Usage."

- Quotation marks are used to emphasize a certain word: The word "permit" is used to indicate authorization.

English and Language Usage

Apostrophes

The apostrophe (') has a few different functions:

- Apostrophes are used to designate a quote within a quote: The professor said, "The word 'circumvent' means to avoid or get around."

- Apostrophes are used for contractions, such as in "can't" or "won't."

- Apostrophes are used to show possession: "Bob's house" or "Veronica's purse."

Example

Q. Which of the following sentences uses correct punctuation?

a. Carole is not currently working; her focus is on her children at the moment.
b. Carole is not currently working and her focus is on her children at the moment.
c. Carole is not currently working, her focus is on her children at the moment.
d. Carole is not currently working her focus is on her children at the moment.

Explanation

Answer. A: Choice *A* is correctly punctuated because it uses a semicolon to join two independent clauses that are related in meaning. Each of these clauses could function as an independent sentence. In Choice *B*, *because* would be a better conjunction choice than *and*. Choice *C* is a comma splice, and Choice *D* is a run-on sentence.

Correct Sentence Structures

A **sentence** is a set of words that make up a grammatical unit. To be a complete sentence, it must at a minimum contain a **subject** and a **verb** and must convey a complete thought.

Sentence Types

There are four types of sentences in the English language.

- **Declarative**: A statement that ends with a period. Declarative sentence are the most common type of sentence: "We are going to the beach this weekend."

- **Imperative**: A command, instruction, or request that ends with a period. The subject of an imperative sentence is **implied**: "Clean your room before we go to the beach."

- **Interrogative**: A question that ends with a question mark: "Are we going to my favorite beach?"

- **Exclamatory**: A statement that expresses some kind of strong emotion that ends with an exclamation mark: "I love going to that beach!"

Sentence Structures

A **simple sentence** has one independent clause: "I am going to win."

A **compound sentence** has two independent clauses. A conjunction—*for*, *and*, *nor*, *but*, *or*, *yet*, *so*—links them together. Note that each of the independent clauses has a subject and a verb and could stand on its own as a complete sentence: "I am going to win, but the odds are against me."

A **complex sentence** has one independent clause and one or more dependent clauses. Dependent clauses cannot stand on their own as complete sentences. Some conjunctions that link an independent and a dependent clause are *although*, *because*, *before*, *after*, *that*, *when*, *which*, and *while*: "I am going to win, even though I don't deserve it."

A **compound-complex sentence** has at least three clauses, two of which are independent and at least one that is a dependent clause: "While trying to dance, I tripped over my partner's feet, but I regained my balance quickly."

Parts of Speech

Words in a sentence are categorized based on their function. The eight parts of speech are described below.

Nouns

A **noun** is a person, place, thing, or idea.

A **common noun** is a word that names general people, places, or things. Examples of common nouns are animals, objects, feelings, actions, qualities, or numbers.

A **proper noun** is a specific name of a person, place, or thing. Examples include names of people, shops, cities, restaurants, churches, banks, or anything with a particular name.

Pronoun

A **pronoun** is a word used in place of a noun.

Personal pronouns refer to people.

- First person: we, I, our, mine
- Second person: you, yours
- Third person: he, them

Possessive pronouns demonstrate ownership (mine, his, hers, its, ours, theirs, yours).

English and Language Usage

Interrogative pronouns ask questions (what, which, who, whom, whose).

Relative pronouns include the five interrogative pronouns and others that are relative (whoever, whomever, that, when, where).

Demonstrative pronouns replace something specific (this, that, those, these).

- **Reciprocal pronouns** indicate something was done or given in return (each other, one another).

- **Indefinite pronouns** have a nonspecific status (anybody, whoever, someone, everybody, somebody).

Adjectives

An **adjective** is a word or phrase that describes a noun or pronoun, naming its characteristics such as size, shape, age color, origin, personality, or type. Adjectives answer the questions *what kind*, *which one*, and *how many*. In the examples below, adjectives are underlined.

- The girl and her <u>amicable</u> dog went to the park.
- Billy's mother went to see a <u>horror</u> movie.

Verbs

The **verb** is the part of speech that describes an action, state of being, or occurrence.

A verb forms the main part of a predicate of a sentence. This means that the verb explains what the noun is doing.

Helping (auxiliary) verbs are words like *have, do, be, can, may, should, must,* and *will*. "I *should* go to the store." Helping verbs assist main verbs in expressing tense, ability, possibility, permission, or obligation.

Verbs have five basic forms: the **base** form, the *-s* form, the *-ing* form, the *past* form, and the **past participle** form.

Adverbs

Adverbs modify or qualify verbs, adjectives, or other adverbs as well as word groups that express a relation of place, time, circumstance, or cause. Adverbs answer the questions *how, when, where, why, in what way, how often, how much, in what condition,* and/or *to what degree*.

Here are some examples of adverbs for different situations:

- how: quickly
- when: daily

English and Language Usage

- where: there
- in what way: easily
- how often: often
- how much: much
- in what condition: badly
- what degree: hardly

Prepositions

Prepositions are connecting words that describe relationships. They are placed before a noun or pronoun, forming a phrase that modifies another word in the sentence. **Prepositional phrases** begin with a preposition and end with a noun or pronoun, the **object of the preposition**: "A pristine lake is <u>near the store</u> and <u>behind the bank</u>." (*Near* and *behind* are prepositions; *store* and *bank* are objects of the prepositions.)

Interjections

Interjections are words used to express emotion. Examples include *wow*, *ouch*, and *hooray*. They are often separated from the rest of the sentence by an exclamation point, comma, or semicolon: "<u>Oh no</u>, I am not going."

Conjunctions

Conjunctions connect words, phrases, thoughts, and ideas to show relationships between components. There are two types: coordinating and subordinating.

Coordinating conjunctions are the primary class of conjunctions placed between words, phrases, clauses, and sentences that are of equal grammatical rank and can stand by themselves as complete sentences. The coordinating conjunctions are *for*, *and*, *nor*, *but*, *or*, *yes*, and *so*: "I need to go shopping, but I must be careful to leave enough money in the bank."

Subordinating conjunctions connect two unequal parts of a sentence, an **independent clause** that can stand by itself as a complete sentence and a **dependent clause** that cannot stand by itself. Notice that the presence of subordinating conjunctions makes clauses dependent: "I must go to the store even though I do not have enough money in the bank."

Possessives

While they are not a separate part of speech, it is important to understand possessives. **Possessive nouns** and **possessive pronouns** show ownership,

Singular nouns are made possessive with an apostrophe and an *s* (*'s*): "My uncle's new car is silver."

Plural nouns ending in *s* are generally made possessive by just adding an apostrophe ('): "The students' achievement tests are difficult."

If the plural noun does not end in an *s* such as *women*, then it is made possessive by adding an *apostrophe s* (*'s*)—*women's*.

Possessive pronouns can be first person (*mine*), second person (*yours*), or third person (*theirs*).

Indefinite possessive pronouns such as *nobody* or *someone* become possessive by adding an *apostrophe s* to become *nobody's* or *someone's*.

Creating Coherent Sentences

Every complete sentence can be divided into two parts: the subject and the predicate.

Subject: who or what the sentence describes.

Simple subjects are the noun or pronouns the sentence describes, without modifiers: "The big brown dog is the calmest one."

Complete subjects are the subject together with all of its describing words or modifiers: "The big brown dog is the calmest one."

Direct subjects are subjects that appear in the text of the sentence, as in the examples above. **Indirect subjects** are implied. The subject is "you," but the word *you* does not appear.

Indirect subjects are usually in imperative sentences that issue a command or order: "Feed the short, skinny dog first. "

Compound subjects occur when two or more nouns join together to form a plural subject: "Carson and Emily make a great couple."

Predicates: Once we have identified the subject of the sentence, the rest of the sentence becomes the predicate. Predicates are formed by the verb, the direct object, and all words related to it: "The gigantic green character was funnier than all the rest."

A **predicate nominative** renames the subject: "John is a carpenter."

English and Language Usage

A **predicate adjective** describes the subject: "Margaret is beautiful."

Direct objects are the nouns in the sentence that are receiving the action: "He gave the pony <u>a soapy bath</u>." (What is being given? a soapy bath)

Indirect objects are words that tell us to or for whom or what the action is being done. For there to be an indirect object, there first must always be a direct object: "He gave <u>the pony</u> a soapy bath." (What is getting the bath? the pony)

Example
Read the sentence below and then answer the question that follows.

Robert needed to find at least four sources for his final project, so he searched several library databases for reliable academic research.

Which words function as nouns in the preceding sentence?
 a. Robert, sources, project, databases, research
 b. Robert, sources, final, project, databases, academic, research
 c. Robert, sources, project, he, library, databases, research
 d. Sources, project, databases, research

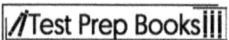
English and Language Usage

Phrases

A **phrase** is a group of words that go together but do not include both a subject and a verb. They add information, explain something, or make the sentence easier for the reader to understand. Unlike clauses, phrases can never stand alone as their own sentences because they do not form complete thoughts. There are noun phrases, prepositional phrases, verbal phrases, appositive phrases, and absolute phrases.

Subject-Verb Agreement

The subject of a sentence and its verb must agree grammatically in number. A singular subject requires a singular verb; a plural subject requires a plural verb

- Incorrect: The houses is new.
- Correct: The houses are new.
- Also Correct: The house is new.

English and Language Usage

Example

Q. Which of the following sentences uses correct subject-verb agreement?

    a. There is two constellations that can be seen from the back of the house.

    b. At least four of the sheep needs to be sheared before the end of summer.

    c. Lots of people were auditioning for the singing competition on Saturday.

    d. Everyone in the group have completed the assignment on time.

Explanation

Answer. C: The simple subject of this sentence, the word *lots*, is plural. It agrees with the plural verb form *were*.

Knowledge of Language

Using Grammar to Enhance Clarity in Writing

Forming Complete Sentences

Independent and dependent clauses are strings of words that contain both a subject and a verb. An **independent clause** *can* stand alone as complete thought, but a **dependent clause** *cannot*. A dependent clause relies on other words to be a complete sentence.

Transitions
Transitions help connect and organize ideas within sentences and paragraphs, between them, and (in longer documents) between sections. Transitions may be single words, sentences, or whole paragraphs.

Verb Tense
Verb tense is used to show when the action in the sentence took place.

Present tense shows the action is happening currently or is ongoing.

Past tense shows that the action happened in the past or that the state of being is in the past.

Future tense shows that the action will happen in the future or is a future state of being.

Present perfect tense shows an action that started in the past but continues into the present.

Past perfect tense shows an action was finished before another took place.

Future perfect tense shows an action that will be completed in the future.

Mood

Mood is used to show the speaker's feelings about the subject matter. In English, there is indicative mood, imperative mood, and subjunctive mood.

Indicative mood is used to state facts, ask questions, or state opinions.

Imperative mood is used to state a command or make a request.

Subjunctive mood is used to express a wish, an opinion, or a hope that is contrary to fact.

Example

Q. After a long day at work, Tracy had dinner with her family, and then took a walk to the park.
What are the transitional words in the preceding sentence?
    a. After, then
    b. At, with, to
    c. Had, took
    d. A, the

Explanation

Answer. A: *After* and *then* are transitional words that indicate time or position. Choice *B* is incorrect because the words *at, with,* and *to* are used as prepositions in this sentence, not transitions. Choice *C* is incorrect because the words *had* and *took* are used as verbs in this sentence. In Choice *D*, *a* and *the* are used as articles in the sentence.

Evaluate if Language Meets the Needs of an Audience for a Provided Rhetorical Context

Formal and Informal Language

Formal language is used in academia or in professional settings. Formal language uses standard English grammar and technical or relevant jargon related to its topic. It avoids contractions, slang, colloquialisms, and first-person pronouns.

Informal language is used to communicate with peers, family members, or friends. It is more concerned with communicating in a friendly or casual manner than with sounding professional. The tone is more relaxed and slang, contractions, clichés, and the first and second person may be used in writing. The imperative voice may be used as well.

Slang refers to non-standard expressions that are not used in elevated speech and writing. Slang creates linguistic in-groups and out-groups of people, those who can understand the slang terms and those who can't. Slang is often tied to a specific time period.

English and Language Usage

Colloquial language is language that is used conversationally or familiarly in contrast to formal, professional, or academic language.

Example

Q. A teacher wants to counsel a student about using the word *ain't* in a research paper for a high school English class. What advice should the teacher give?

    a. *Ain't* is not in the dictionary, so it isn't a word.
    b. Because the student isn't in college yet, *ain't* is an appropriate expression for a high school writer.
    c. *Ain't* is incorrect English and should not be part of a serious student's vocabulary because it sounds uneducated.
    d. *Ain't* is a colloquial expression, and while it may be appropriate in a conversational setting, it is not standard in academic writing.

Explanation

Answer. D: Colloquial language is that which is used conversationally or informally, in contrast to professional or academic language.

Develop a Well-Organized Paragraph

A good **paragraph** should have the following characteristics:

- Be logical with organized sentences
- Have a unified purpose within itself
- Use sentences as building blocks
- Be a distinct section of a piece of writing
- Present a single theme introduced by a topic sentence
- Maintain a consistent flow through subsequent, relevant, well-placed sentences
- Tell a story of its own or have its own purpose, yet connect with what is written before and after
- Enlighten, entertain, and/or inform
- Additionally, paragraphs should be coherent, which is the quality of being logical and consistent. Elements of coherence include a topic sentence, logical order, consistency, transitions, and good grammar.

English and Language Usage

Example

Examine the following two paragraphs, each an example of a movie review. Read them and form a critique.

Example 1: *Eddie the Eagle* is a movie about a struggling athlete. Eddie was crippled at birth. He had a lot of therapy and he had a dream. Eddie trained himself for the Olympics. He went far away to learn how to ski jump. It was hard for him, but he persevered. He got a coach and kept trying. He qualified for the Olympics. He was the only one from Britain who could jump. When he succeeded, they named him, "Eddie the Eagle."

Example 2: The last movie I saw in the theater was *Eddie the Eagle,* a story of extraordinary perseverance inspired by real life events. Eddie was born in England with a birth defect that he slowly but surely overcame, but not without trial and error (not the least of which was his father's perpetual *dis*couragement). In fact, the old man did everything to get him to give up, but Eddie was dogged beyond anyone in the neighborhood; in fact, maybe beyond anyone in the whole town or even the whole world! Eddie, simply, did not know to quit. As he grew up, so did his dream; a strange one, indeed, for someone so unaccomplished: to compete in the Winter Olympics as a ski jumper (which he knew absolutely nothing about). Eddie didn't just keep on dreaming about it. He actually went to Germany and *worked* at it, facing unbelievable odds, defeats, and put-downs by Dad and the other Men in Charge, aka the Olympic decision-makers. Did that stop him? No way! Eddie got a coach and persevered. Then, when he failed, he persevered some more, again and again. You should be able to open up a dictionary, look at the word "persevere," and see a picture of Eddie the Eagle because, when everybody told him he couldn't, he did. The result? He is forever dubbed, "Eddie the Eagle."

Explanation

Both reviews tell something about the movie *Eddie the Eagle*. Does one motivate the reader to want to see the movie more than the other? The second review uses a more passionate tone and figurative language to better appeal to the audience.

Using Language and Vocabulary to Express Ideas in Writing

Apply Basic Knowledge of the Elements of the Writing Process to Communicate Effectively

The most important parts of the writing process are planning (brainstorming, outlining, free writing), writing, referencing sources, and revising.

Planning

Brainstorming: Before beginning a draft, a writer should always take a few moments to think about the topic and jot down any immediate ideas that could work for the essay. This process, called brainstorming, is a way to get some words on the page and offer a reference for ideas when drafting.

Outlining: An **outline** is a system used to organize writing. Usually, outlines start out with the main idea(s) and then branch out into subgroups or subsidiary thoughts or subjects. Outlines provide a visual tool to see how key parts of an essay or text relate to one another. An example of a standard five-paragraph essay outline is below, although essays should always be organized according to the writer's information.

    I. Introduction
    II. Main Topic 1
        a. Subtopic 1
        b. Subtopic 2
            1. Detail 1
            2. Detail 2
    III. Main Topic 2
        a. Subtopic 1
            1. Detail 1
            2. Detail 2
        b. Subtopic 2
    IV. Main Topic 3
        a. Subtopic 1
            1. Detail 1
        b. Subtopic 2
            1. Detail 1
    V. Conclusion

Free Writing: Like brainstorming, free writing is designed to help the writer generate ideas. This method involves setting a timer for two or three minutes and writing down all ideas that come to mind about the topic using complete sentences. Once time is up, review the sentences to see what observations have been made and how these ideas might translate into a more coherent direction for the topic.

Writing

Writing is when the essay is actually put together. The writing, or drafting, process should follow the outline closely, so the passage doesn't get cluttered. Remember that your work here does not have to be perfect. This process is often referred to as **drafting** because you're just creating a rough draft of your work.

Referencing Sources

Anytime you quote or paraphrase another piece of writing you will need to include a **citation**. A citation is a short description of the work that your quote or information came from. The manual of style your teacher or employer wants you to follow will dictate exactly how to format that citation. Common style manuals include APA, MLA, or Chicago style. If using direct quotes, writers should always use quotation marks.

Revising

Revising and proofreading offers an opportunity for writers to polish their essays and fix any issues. Read the entire paper and check for confusing syntax, jumbled organization, incomplete arguments, etc. Rewrite where needed. Then, check the paper once more for any grammatical mistakes. This will ensure the essay will be presented at its best.

English and Language Usage

Example

Rewrite the sentence, following the directions given below.

Q. Seasoned runners often advise new runners to get fitted for better quality running shoes because new runners often complain about minor injuries like sore knees or shin splints.

> Rewrite, beginning with <u>Seasoned runners often advise new runners to get fitted for better quality running shoes</u>. The next words will be which of the following:
>
> a. to help them avoid minor injuries
> b. because they know better
> c. , so they can run further
> d. to complain about running injuries

Explanation

Answer. A: This answer best matches the meaning of the original sentence, which states that seasoned runners offer advice to new runners because they have complaints of injuries. Choice *B* may be true, but it doesn't mention the complaints of injuries by new runners. Choice *C* may also be true, but it does not match the original meaning of the sentence. Choice *D* does not make sense in the context of the sentence.

Determine the Meaning of Words by Analyzing Word Parts

By analyzing and understanding Latin, Greek, and Anglo-Saxon word roots, prefixes, and suffixes one can better understand word meanings.

A word can consist of the following:

- root
- root + suffix
- prefix + root
- prefix + root + suffix

Roots are the basic components of words.

A **prefix** is a word, letter, or number that is placed before another. It adjusts or qualifies the root word's meaning.

A **suffix** is a letter or group of letters added at the end of a word to form another word. The word created from the root and suffix is either a different tense of the same root (*help + ed = helped*) or a new word (*help + ful = helpful*).

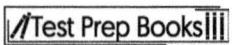 **English and Language Usage**

Example
Q. Glorify, fortify, gentrify, acidify

Based on the preceding words, what is the correct meaning of the suffix –*fy*?
   a. Marked by, given to
   b. Doer, believer
   c. Make, cause, cause to have
   d. Process, state, rank

Explanation
Answer. C: The suffix -*fy* means to make, cause, or cause to have. Choices *A, B,* and *D* are incorrect because they show meanings of other suffixes. Choice *A* shows the meaning of the suffix -*ous*. Choice *B* shows the meaning of the suffix –*ist*, and Choice *D* shows the meaning of the suffix -*age*.

FREE Test Taking Tips Video/DVD Offer

To better serve you, we created videos covering test taking tips that we want to give you for FREE. **These videos cover world-class tips that will help you succeed on your test.**

We just ask that you send us feedback about this product. Please let us know what you thought about it—whether good, bad, or indifferent.

To get your **FREE videos**, you can use the QR code below or email freevideos@studyguideteam.com with "Free Videos" in the subject line and the following information in the body of the email:

    a. The title of your product

    b. Your product rating on a scale of 1-5, with 5 being the highest

    c. Your feedback about the product

If you have any questions or concerns, please don't hesitate to contact us at info@studyguideteam.com.

Thank you!

www.ingramcontent.com/pod-product-compliance
Lightning Source LLC
Chambersburg PA
CBHW071440150426
43191CB00008B/1187